ADVERTISING

· PORTFOLIO ·

Creating an Effective Presentation of Your Work

Ann Marie Barry

D0620081

NTC Business Books

a division of *NTC Publishing Group* • Lincolnwood, Illinois USA

To Peter Seward and Eileen Barry with love

Published by NTC Business Books, a division of NTC Publishing Group.
© 1990 by NTC Publishing Group, 4255 West Touhy Avenue,
Lincolnwood (Chicago), Illinois 60646-1975 U.S.A.
Manufactured in the United States of America.
Library of Congress Catalog Card Number 89-60323

0 VP 9 8 7 6 5 4 3 2

Contents

Illustrations

A Note from the Author

Dear Reader,

While lack of education or experience presents a significant handicap, neither of these need prevent you from building an effective portfolio—if you realize that study cannot substitute for talent nor talent for experience. You simply need all three.

Begin by listening to what the most successful people in advertising have to say. The advice of advertising geniuses such as David Ogilvy and Leo Burnett is in print. Copywriters such as John Caples and Claude Hopkins have told us their secrets. Take the time to read and learn them.

You will also have to know something about layout and the tools that you will need to produce ads. Again, excellent books are available, and if you are lucky enough to be in a work situation where you have access to the best equipment, use it and ask questions of the creative people around you on the human, technical, and creative problems which challenge their best work.

Local metropolitan advertising clubs and organizations, like the Ad Club of Greater Boston, the nation's oldest; national publications like *Advertising Age* and *ADWEEK;* and organizations like the American Association of Advertising Agencies (4 A's), the Business/ Professional Advertising Association (B/PAA), and others also offer excellent workshops and seminars taught by professionals in the field on specific aspects of creative and account services work.

Attend organizational meetings, volunteer to hang work for professional advertising competitions, ask questions, listen to conversations, and get as much practical experience related to creative advertising work as you can. Opportunities always seem to open for talent and persistence.

Above all, when you finally have your "book" together, listen more and take advice on what's effective and what isn't from people in the field who interview you, especially if there is no chance of getting a job from the interview. Remember, however, that opinions may vary. Be persistent and prepared to hear conflicting advice, but listen for the patterns and test what you hear against your own developing creative judgment.

The following book is intended as a practical guide for the novice who is short on experience but intent on putting together a creative portfolio and getting into advertising. In it you will find practical information, professional advice, and some specific suggestions from the country's top ad agency creative directors. It doesn't pretend to have all the answers or to contain a secret formula for making your creative portfolio an instant "knockout." Your own determination, creativity, depth of thought, and specific research will do that.

When you have read and mastered the basic concepts and principles included in the text and in the "Suggested Readings," you will then be ready to follow the first and most important rule of advertising. Neil Vanover, senior partner and executive creative director of Tatham-Laird & Kudner, sums it up clearly and succinctly: "Learn all the rules, then forget all the rules. Read all the books about how to put your book together and then do it better than that. Do it better than your professors tell you to do it. Cut through. This is not a business of filling out forms. Invent a new form. Play your own game, a game of your own invention and then nobody can do it better than you can."

I hope this book helps you get started. My sincerest best wishes for your success.

Ann Marie Barry

Acknowledgments

A sincere thank you to the following people for their kind help and advice:

Robert Montgomery and Walter Lubars of Boston University • Ted Bell of Leo Burnett USA • Dennis Bruce of Miller Myers Bruce Dalla Costa • Carl Casselman of Jordan, McGrath, Case & Taylor • John Chervokas of Sudler & Hennessey • Dextor Fedor of The Bloom Agency • Frank Ginsberg of Avrett, Free & Ginsberg • Marta Greenbaum of Telephone Marketing Programs, Inc. • Harvey Gabor of Ingalls, Quinn & Johnson • James Herringshaw of Nationwide Advertising Service • Paul Hodges of Laurence, Charles, Free & Lawson • Harry Jacobs of The Martin Agency • Paul Keye of keye/donna/pearlstein • Ken Lavey of Lavey/Wolff/Swift • Bill Lunsford of The Weightman Group • Louis Miano of AC&R/DHB & Bess • Joe McNeil of Ross Roy Group • David Moore of Stone & Adler • Dick Pantano of Hill, Holiday, Connors, Cosmopulos • Leslie E. Parker, Jr., of Tucker Wayne/Luckie & Co. • Susan Puzzuoli of McCann-Erickson NY-/Worldwide • Doug Rucker of Richards Group • Al Samuelson of Keller-Crescent • Emily Soell of Rapp & Collins USA • Nancy Temkin of J. Walter Thompson • Neil Vanover of Tatham-Laird & Kudner • Robert Bissell • Nancy Carroll • Donna and Stan Freberg • James Grant • Stella Smith • Tim Younkin • Elizabeth MacDonell and Cas Psujek of NTC

1

The Advertising Creative Portfolio
What It Is and What It Should Have in It

First, about Your Portfolio

When you apply for a job in "Creative," you will probably be asked if you have a "book"—that is, a portfolio which contains a compilation of your best creative work in advertising. Your work may be speculative ads that have never appeared in print, focusing on a variety of existent or nonexistent products and/or services; or it may be a collection of creative work done free lance or while working for an ad agency or other organization. Your portfolio will probably consist of both, to show what you have done and also what you can do, if left entirely to your own creative devices.

If you are a student, you will probably be putting together a book which is mostly speculative, but if you have done work during an advertising internship which got a lot of compliments, you will probably want to include that also. If you are already in the open job market or working in a related communications field, you may have samples of design or copy work that you've had a hand in and which eventually ended up in print. Whatever material you choose to include, you will want to present it in the best possible light.

For this purpose, you will want to buy a portfolio case from any good graphic arts supply store, preferably one with protective acetate leaves which opens on three sides like a book. It should be in a size manageable enough to carry around and to be placed comfortably on a desktop for study, but large

1

enough to hold your creative work once it's been mounted with a two- to three-inch border.

Or you can mount your ads on black mat board or rigid foam panels and leave them loose in a hard case, ready to leaf through. If you do this, then you'll need to cover the ads with acetate from a roll (just clip the excess from the corners and tape in back), which is also available at an art supply store.

There are a variety of styles, sizes, and prices for the different cases, each designed to accommodate varying needs and tastes, so you'll have a considerable number of choices. Select the creative work you want to include before you buy your portfolio case, so you'll be sure it will suit your needs.

Creative judgment

The purpose of the portfolio or "book" is simple. When complete, it does what no résumé can: it shows the quality of your imagination and the variety of advertising work that you are capable of doing. Your portfolio will be reviewed by a creative director, art director, or copywriter in the ad agency or on the client-side, who will decide to hire you or not in part based on the work you present.

Walter Lubars, former senior copywriter at Doyle Dane Bernbach and creative supervisor for J. Walter Thompson, now at Boston University, reminds us that each ad must do three basic things:

First, it must get noticed.   This implies developing an approach or attention-getting device relevant to the product or service.

Second, it must hold attention   long enough to get the selling message across. This means making the product inherently interesting to a person who may find it useful.

Third, it must be memorable   enough to be recalled when the potential consumer is making the buying decision—whether in advance if it is an expensive item, or at the point of purchase, if it falls into the category of those 80 percent of all goods which are subject to impulse purchasing in the store.

In judging your ability to create ads that accomplish these three basic criteria, the creative director reviewing your book will be looking for

- creative imagination and talent for innovative work;

- professionalism in handling materials;

- design sense, layout ability, typography choices;

- ability to grab reader attention and break through ad clutter;

- fresh, original, strong, clear, convincing, succinct and error-free body copy;

- knowledgeability about the product or service;

- ability to visualize and verbalize product benefit;

- strength in strategic and conceptual thinking;

- full and logical development of clear, concise concepts;

- creative ideas with enough breadth and depth to be translated into a whole campaign and a variety of media;

- knowledge of target market and media characteristics.

Consider creative strategy first

Have a well developed creative strategy for each ad which shows an understanding of marketing concepts and persuasion techniques. For each individual ad and each campaign in your portfolio, you should be able to define the

- ad or campaign objective,

- target market,

- key consumer benefit,

- reasons which support its credibility,

- long-term "personality" to be developed for the product,

- rationale for the creative approach and the direction of future campaigns.

If the ad is truly an effective one, it will already contain or suggest all of these, because you will have had to determine them before doing any creative execution. (See Illustration 1.1 on pages 10–11 for a planning breakdown of these elements.)

Joe McNeil, executive creative director for the Ross Roy Group, says that ad strategy is the most important thing he looks for in a creative book: "If the ad is the answer to a client's advertising/communication problem, how did you arrive at the solution? What thinking was involved? How will the message solve the problem?'' A good "spec" presentation, he says, is one that demonstrates exactly how the agency can solve a creative problem, is translatable into all media, and develops out of a solid knowledge of the product, the market, and the budget.

What Your Book Should Have in It

When your book is being reviewed, you may be there to explain how and why you took certain approaches or made certain decisions, or you may be asked to leave it for a few days. In either case, your creative work will have to stand on its own merits; your ads will have to be self-explanatory, just as they must be when published. If you have other appointments and can't leave your whole book, be prepared with black-and-white or color copies of your best work (either by photo or photocopy) so that these can be left along with your résumé.

Because your book must speak for itself, it is important not only that you make the right decisions as you create your ads, but also that you make the right choices on what to include in your book as a whole.

Dextor Fedor, senior vice president and creative director of The Bloom Agency, emphasizes that effective creative books are characterized by high creativity, consistency, follow-through, clear, concise concepts, simplicity in communicating them, and solid ideas that make sense. The book must be "carefully and attentively assembled," he states, and follow a deliberately chosen creative strategy.

His insights were echoed in a recent survey of creative directors in the country's largest 100 advertising agencies. These top creatives were asked to identify and comment on the most common mistakes made by novices in creating individual ads and in building their creative portfolios.

Among the most common mistakes cited were

- including too much material in the portfolio and not being selective enough in the quality of the work included;

- lack of marketing awareness and knowledge of product, target market, competitive environment, and budget concerns;

- lack of a well thought-out, fully developed, logically integrated, and consistent creative strategy;

- talking to themselves or their peers instead of to the real target market for the product;

- reliance on imitation or outright "theft" of creative ideas as a substitute for original concepts, especially imitating other ads, following creative fads, and straining for cleverness in plays on words or cheap puns;

- poor presentation of ads, from inept lettering to sloppy renderings and layouts, to clutter and illegible copy;

- poor integration of elements—i.e., visuals and heads which are intrinsically unrelated to each other or to the body copy, or only some or none of these related to the product itself.

In view of these criticisms, the following suggestions may simplify the process of building your creative portfolio:

Limit the number of pieces you include

Keep the highest standards for your work and your selections. If you have only five or six excellent pieces, limit your selection to them. A professional evaluating your book will be able to tell very quickly how good you really are. David Ogilvy asked potential hirees to send him only six of their best pieces.

James Herringshaw, creative director for Nationwide Advertising Service, agrees that the right six pieces can reveal the full range of a person's creative ability, and he reminds the novice that although "ideas, thought process and innovative talent come first" in a portfolio, "presentation is important. Keep it brief." About **twelve to fifteen pieces** are probably ideal—more than twenty can only be redundant.

Never put in pieces just to cover a category or fatten the book. As your book grows, weed out the lesser pieces and keep only the most outstanding ones. Continually revise; never consider your book as finally "finished."

Bill Lunsford, senior vice president and creative director of The Weightman Group, comments practically and sympathetically that "some of the things you love will have to go or you'll show too much. Never believe it's finished. Keep working on it. Build it, stay away from it awhile, and then go back to it." If the creative concept still seems strategically sound and involving, and the ad seems to sell itself, then it's probably good enough to leave in.

Above all, put in only your best work

As you review your work, remember that the person who sees your book will assume that you think that everything in it is terrific. **Putting in things that you think are just "okay" or even "good" will lead your reviewer to**

conclude that either you don't discriminate or you think mediocre work is excellent. Neither one of these conclusions will get you back for a second interview, and they certainly won't get you a job.

Doug Rucker, creative director of The Richards Group, gives this advice: "Make sure that you are confident every piece in your book reflects the very best you can do, that every headline/visual makes people think about the product/service you are advertising in an interesting new way. If not, don't include it."

When deciding on work in which you have had a substantial part and which has been used by an agency for a client, include only the best, with a brief label stating what you were responsible for. Don't go into lengthy explanations, however, and never take credit for work you didn't do. As always, be prepared to discuss the evolution of each piece.

Include ads for a variety of products

Because you'll have to be versatile in your agency work, make your book look as versatile as you're expected to be. Choose a broad range of products and services with a variety of target markets and advertising appeals. The more diverse, the better.

Don't choose products or services that are already overexposed in the media, and don't automatically select the first topics that come to mind. To stand out from the crowd, you must never sound like other ads or labor on worked-over products or issues. Avoid eccentricity as well. Make your creative approach, not the product, unique.

Choose products that are difficult to advertise, like cabbage, automobile tires, or vinegar. John Chervokas, executive vice president and chief creative officer of Sudler & Hennessey, suggests replacing a Budweiser ad with one for Montana beef, an ad for Bermuda tourism with one for Afghanistan.

The principle is simply that your creativity will show more when the product has less inherent appeal. If your approach or content is generically familiar, your ad will not muster enough interest to break through the clutter—especially of other people's creative books.

Consider both your own talent and what the creative director wants to see

Your different creative approaches should arise naturally out of the variety of products you choose, but never use variety simply for its own sake. If you are strong in a particular area—like photography, drawing or sketching, do ads that lend themselves to this execution and stress it in your portfolio. This is the place to stretch and advertise your talent. If you have it, show it.

Also be aware that each medium—photography, line drawing, pastel, watercolor, oils—has its own personality which will rub off on the product. Food ads may require four-color photography to capture food's sensual appeal, but a combination watercolor/pen-and-ink drawing can establish the perfect light tone for a plant hospital ad. Make the medium of execution reflect the character of the product as you choose items, services, and mediums which display your creative talent.

Some creative directors, like Marta Greenbaum of Telephone Marketing Programs, Inc., the largest Yellow Pages agency in the world, suggest gearing your portfolio to each interview by finding out about the company first and then tailoring the ads included toward what the creative director wants to see. This is especially important in terms of the type of client a company serves and the media in which it may specialize.

Paul Keye, chairman and creative director of keye/donna/pearlstein, says it's really just a matter of good manners: "Know whom you're presenting to. If it's an agency, know its reputation and self-image, its clients, and its work. Advertising agencies are run by egocentric, preoccupied people. If you have some idea of what they're doing and why, you'll present yourself and your work in that context. It's nothing deceitful or phony; just good manners."

Joe McNeil of Ross Roy even advises preparing speculative ads on products for which the agency is famous in order to "demonstrate exactly how you can help that agency solve a creative problem, in all media."

In addition to being daring and the true acid test of your creative work, McNeil feels, such ads have the primary advantage of clearly showing your interest in the agency. And although your work may not equal the agency's own, it gives you an opportunity for a more focused, in-depth, and intelligent discussion in an area of common creative ground.

Include ads for several campaigns

While the individual pieces of the ad campaign will focus on the same product and benefit, reflecting the same theme and approach, each will state the case in a different way, reflecting the limitations and benefits of the medium.

The illustration, headline, and copy of each campaign piece must be independent of other ads in the series, however. You can't assume carryover from a previous ad or an ongoing familiarity with the individual product or its benefit. Think of each ad as the first one your target market will see.

A practical approach to each campaign is to take a single product with a single benefit focus and do a series of treatments which utilize different media, chosen by the potential exposure of your target market to them. In a single page write-up before each campaign (but not each ad), briefly identify the product and explain its positioning, describe the potential consumer and outline your creative strategy and its rationale. (See Illustration 1.1, "Ad Campaign Planning Guide," for a breakdown of these.)

You may decide to include an outline based on the planning sheet with each campaign in your portfolio, but just the fact that you have done this before creating each ad will keep you on target with a consistent creative strategy. The strategy will then show in each ad you create, and you will be prepared to explain it in an interview.

Include at least two campaigns in your portfolio, preferably in different media. Because campaigns are more difficult to do than single ads, they will tell more about your creative ability. Although most candidates for an advertising job can develop a clever idea for at least one ad, coming up with an idea deep and strong enough to be sustained through a campaign is one test of a truly creative person.

See the *Field & Stream* campaign (Illustrations 5.7–5.10) in Chapter 5 for an excellent example of how such a campaign can develop and prosper.

Matching the creative execution and media with the product image, ad budget, and target market

Be sure that each media choice is appropriate for the product's image, and that it's likely to reach potential consumers as they go through their everyday routine. If your target market drives to work, consider radio. If they take rapid transit, consider car cards. If they are likely to work at home, consider direct mail or newspapers.

Whatever media are best suited to your target market, however, keep in mind the probable budget when you plan your ads. Don't use executions that involve needless expense, and make sure that the personality of the product, your target market, and the media are all compatible.

Check media characteristics to be sure sizes are to scale and that production techniques can accommodate your ideas—e.g., be aware that outdoor posters and "paints" (painted bulletins) differ in size; different newspapers have different color capabilities and policies.

And be sure that the typeface, amount of copy, and the size and complexity of the illustration are appropriate for the limitations and advantages of each chosen medium. For example, outdoor posters cannot accommodate large amounts of body copy or complex illustrations, while magazine ads can handle a lot of information or explanation. On the other hand, highly detailed sketches won't work in small newspaper ads.

For your "spec" ads, you may want to begin with the product, benefit, and target market. Then choose the medium according to its characteristics, editorial environment, and ability to reach the target market. Or you may work in reverse, choosing the media first and then the product and target on the basis of the media characteristics.

Include a variety of media and creative executions

To showcase your image and copy versatility, you will want to consider including some or all of the following:

- black-and-white newspaper ad
- two- or three-color newspaper ad
- one-half page or less four-color magazine ad
- four-color bleed magazine ad
- outdoor poster or painted bulletin
- indoor car card
- 30-second radio commercial
- direct mail piece, with two follow-up pieces
- two-page catalog spread
- two to three ad campaigns, with three to four pieces in each

If you are familiar with television production and feel that television is an important part of the campaign you envision, you may also wish to include a television storyboard of a 15-second or 30-second commercial. If you do, be sure to use proper storyboard format, and always keep in mind the advantages and limitations of the medium in relation to your strategy and product message.

Ad Campaign Planning Guide

1. Product/Service
Name the product and generically describe what it is.

2. Key Product Benefit
Decide and state the most meaningful reason for your target market to buy the product. Name and benefit will be combined in the ad headline.

3. Target Market
Construct a brief consumer profile:

demographically—all the vital statistics that describe the consumer in terms of age, sex, income, education, children, ownership of goods, home, etc.;

psychographically—the kind of attitudes, values and life-style the consumer has; what he or she cares about and spends time and money on.

4. Supporting Information
Make a list of specific facts about the product and your consumer's use of it in relation to the key benefit. Include all relevant data first and then reduce data to the key information necessary to personally convince the consumer of the product's benefit. Together with the emotional and psychological appeal, these facts will form the body copy.

5. Emotional Appeal
Conveyed through choice of subject itself, ad illustration, word choice in the copy and headlines, general tone and approach to the subject, the emotional appeal gives the consumer a psychologically fulfilling reason for buying the product.

How you want the consumer to feel about himself or herself through using the product will give you direction for the proper appeal. The ratio and emphasis of "how many facts" to "how much feeling" depends on the consumer's acceptance of the product, his or her satisfaction with its practical utility, and his or her ego involvement with the product image and in experiencing the product itself.

6. Campaign Objective

State exactly what you wish to communicate to the target market about the product through the advertising message. Keep it simple, framed in terms of how you wish the consumer to act, think, and feel in relation to the product.

7. Product Image

This is a brief description of how you wish the public to view your product and its personality over the long run. Each ad must consciously work toward building product acceptance through this image.

8. Creative Strategy

Explain the most effective creative approach to reach the target market, establish product personality, and achieve the communication objective. Include a statement of, and rationale for, your chosen emotional and psychological appeal and creative approach. Explain how and why you think your particular approach and creative executions will work.

(Is a serious, straightforward, factual approach to the product benefit in order? Or is your audience going to be more susceptible to a light, almost whimsical approach? Is the approach consistent with the product image? Can the main theme be executed in a variety of creative formats?)

9. Media Choices

List your primary media choices, with a brief explanation of why each particular medium is appropriate to the product, target market, campaign objective, and creative strategy.

Illustration 1.1   Ad Campaign Planning Guide. Decisions must be made before doing the creative execution.

Although your portfolio may not include all the media listed here, you will probably want to include as full a range as is practical, because an understanding of how each medium shapes its message is essential to effective advertising. You may want to tailor the media to your chosen agency's interests if they are media-specific. Before doing any creative executions, review Chapter 5, "The Message Needs a Medium," which includes a discussion of basic media characteristics.

Consider expanding or revising existing ads

You may also decide to expand an existing ad into a compatible original campaign or to redo an ad campaign that isn't effective. You can show how good you are by recognizing a great ad when you see one and then by making another just as good to build a series. You can show your talent also by turning a poor ad into a good one. When you criticize, however, make sure that you are on solid ground; and when you build on an ad, be sure the original idea was worthy of it.

If you redo an existing campaign, make sure you know who did the campaign, that you understand exactly what the campaign was trying to do, who it was trying to reach, and what the creative strategy was. When you change something, do it only out of knowledge and creative spark, and be sure your alterations are extensive and important enough to be warranted.

In presenting contrasting campaigns, place the ineffective ad(s) first, with a succinct list of its mistakes/weaknesses either on a page placed opposite or just behind but easily accessible. Follow this with your own work, which should clearly and obviously correct the weaknesses and improve the strategy and creative execution. And while you're at it, make sure that you don't commit *other* errors yourself.

2

What Your Book Should Leave Out

What you leave out of your book is almost as important as the work you put in.

Leave out everything that isn't your best work

Do not use two or more single ads for the same product. Present only the best and leave the others out. The same is true of ad campaigns for the same product. Invariably, the person who reviews your book will compare the ads and see one as better. Why lose if you don't have to?

This caution does not apply, however, to follow-up campaigns or to a repositioning of your product to a new user, a new use, or more use in the future. But when you do this, make sure that the successive ad or campaign fully complements the original one and that they're both equally strong in impact. Work for a consistent product image and interesting variations on the central theme, but don't change the tone or violate the original product personality.

Build on what you have done before, shifting the focus, but don't undo previous good work. Rebuilding an image you have already established is wasteful and unnecessary, and can be avoided if you plan well in the beginning. However, always feel free to change anything and everything that is ineffective in an existing ad or campaign which you reposition as part of your "spec" work.

Omit or redo any work that isn't "clean"

Don't put in classroom material containing corrections or comments. Never let errors, smudges, glue, peeling tape, stray marks, lifting letters, etc., stay as they are. If you can't remove or fix what's wrong, then redo the entire thing or use opaque white, matching tape, or whatever works to cover. Then photocopy the material in black and white or color.

Crisp, neat, clean, clear executions are high on the priority list of top creative directors. Don't confuse "rough" with sloppy, and remember that for many creative directors, neatness and organization are the first indication of disciplined thinking and a sense of professionalism.

Always check on any doubtful punctuation, spelling, and syntax, and never let an error of any kind stand

Misspellings, misreadings, and misstatements make creative directors very nervous, for very good reason. When you have spare time, read a good grammar book and sensitize yourself to common problems, like dangling participial phrases and references without antecedents.

Always keep a dictionary, a thesaurus, and a good grammar and style book on hand when writing and checking copy. And before you pronounce your book ready, make sure someone else—someone with proven grammatical, spelling and punctuation skills—has proofread all of your material.

Leave out academic writing not implicitly related to advertising

Although you can and should include writing samples if you are interested in copywriting, these should be chosen on the basis of the kind of writing you'll be expected to do on the job.

Formal thesis writing, research papers, and themes have much in common with good copywriting: they adhere to basic grammar and punctuation rules, retain proper word usage and syntax; but they require different styles and approaches. Many of the things that seem "taboo" in thesis writing are considered good practice in copywriting—including keeping an informal, personalized approach and tone, conversational wording and exposition.

Errors that might seem minor in contrast to larger idea development in formal thesis writing, can, however, appear major in ad copy and can strike horror into the hearts of creative directors and clients—e.g., spelling the name of the client or product wrong. Don't be cavalier about even the smallest of errors. They'll look very big to the client who is paying for name and product recognition. Although agencies always use proofreaders, don't count on someone else to catch your mistakes. Make sure you look as professional as you're expected to be.

Leave out what is considered "creative writing" in the English class—like poetry and short stories—and always remember that copywriting is its own discipline. Other types of writing will be seen as irrelevant to the job. Material you include should be either original copy or copy rewrites of poorly written ads.

Emily Soell, executive creative director of Rapp & Collins USA, laments that the most common error she sees in novice creative books is "including *everything* they've created, from school newspaper articles, to want ads, to poetry." She advises using "spec" work instead when real experience is thin: "one, two or three great ads are better than one hundred pieces of scrap." Exactly.

Be sensitive to these differences in purpose and style, and if you choose to include more than copywriting in your portfolio, keep it to a minimum.

In general, leave out television storyboards, unless you have experience and the storyboard is an integral part of an ad campaign

Writing for television is a highly specialized area, so be sure you have an understanding of film or video production before you attempt a storyboard. Terms are highly specialized, and there are major limitations imposed by visual media which may not be obvious without some study.

Know the agency's work and focus before you interview. Include storyboards and video/film scripts only if you know the agency will want to see them or if they are a significant adjunct to the other print media you show. The creative director usually will expect to see only print ads, direct mail pieces, and radio commercials.

Leave out ads dependent on image or mood for their "sell"

Ads for cigarettes, liquor, perfume, cola, jeans, etc., either have benefits already too well known, or don't have any substantial benefit at all. Once you have found or drawn or photographed a forceful visual for the product, the creative work is done. Therefore you're not showing the full range of your abilities. Unless you have a brilliant idea and a truly original approach, your ad will look only like a variation on a very common theme. Don't waste the space.

Never include an ad that does not stress a positive and specific benefit meaningful to the consumer

Remember that

- it's the consumer who must see the benefit as meaningful, and to emphasize the right benefit you must get into the thinking of the person buying the product;

- negative approaches usually work only with relief of "suffering points" (selling promises which solve a problem, like chapped lips, as opposed to enhancing a situation or present a benefit, like another flavor or color to choose from);

- people often only glance at ads and therefore may not see the "no" in the headline—a situation that can leave the opposite impression from what you intended;

- the product benefit you stress should be applicable to your product alone and not to your competitors' products as well.

A major problem cited by many creative directors is the tendency of many advertising novices to "talk to themselves," or only to other creatives. Also, novices tend not to see their work as "an uninvolved consumer would." They forget "who the client is," "lose focus," and consequently do not make the appeal relevant to the consumer. The result is a weak creative strategy and an approach that is often more imitative of other ads or fads than it is original or convincing.

Leave out ads that are in poor or questionable taste, make negative assumptions about groups of people, or use a "sex sell"

The easiest way to stop people from listening to you is to offend them. Because people have different standards of taste, measure carefully the characteristics of your target market and don't exclude potential customers from it.

Pay very careful attention to sexist and racist attitudes and treatments that may creep in because you are used to hearing or seeing them, but that are nevertheless offensive. This extends to less obvious groups like mothers-in-law, the mentally retarded, or the physically handicapped. Always take the consumer's dignity and values seriously, and never use language appropriate only to special circumstances or to a small section of your target market. Know the exact denotative and connotative meanings of the words you use.

Sex, to work as a basic appeal, must be clearly and specifically related to the product. I strongly suggest not using it in your "spec" book—it's the cheapest way of getting attention and the surest way of losing it in relation to your product.

If your product has a discernible benefit, show it.

Leave out or rewrite ads that don't speak clearly and directly to your target market

Don't talk down to your audience, or use technical jargon or any word that may not be generally understood.

Here again, beware of sexist or racist stereotyping and of buying into faulty assumptions about intelligence. Jargon excludes people, but if you can explain or educate your audience to a new meaning or a new use, do it. It can be an effective approach, enhancing a positive reader response, *if* you respect your readers and speak to them as equals.

Make your technical and business-to-business ads understandable to the creative director. Because the director is your immediate audience and the one who's going to hire you, don't include an ad written for too specialized an audience, even if it's appropriately targeted. Or rewrite it with the interviewer in mind.

Leave out or rewrite ads that exaggerate or tax credibility

Because most people are naturally skeptical of advertising promises, you must be especially careful not to overstate the case for your product or to use clichéd superlatives to describe it. For credibililty's sake, it is better to slightly understate the case than to overstate it. Then the consumer won't be disappointed in the product's performance and may even be pleasantly surprised.

Similarly, don't let exclamation points creep into headlines or copy, and don't use qualifiers that are either meaningless or lazy or both, like "very" or "most." As a novice, you might consider dropping "unique" from your vocabulary altogether. If your product really is unique—that is, "one of a kind"—it cannot have a comparative qualifier, like "more" or "most."

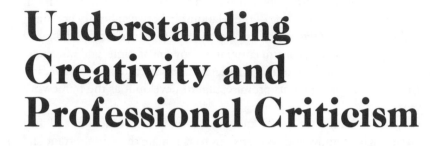

Understanding Creativity and Professional Criticism

What Is Creativity and How Can I Get Some?

Most creative directors agree that you can't teach someone creativity. You can identify it, characterize it, support it, or destroy it. But you can't teach it. Companies that specialize in creativity disagree, but for the most part, they work on unblocking one's natural creativity by establishing situations and promoting dialogue to let the mind roam as freely as it did in childhood.

Although the willingness to make wild associations, and to not let the imagination be checked by inhibition or negative feedback are essential to the functioning of the creative mind, most ad people feel that with high-level creativity you have it or you don't.

There *is* a characteristic profile, however. Really successful creative people have a good sense of humor, a vivid imagination, and a deep interest in people and what motivates them. Their minds traverse a variety of subjects, such as literature, art, history, music, science, and politics. They see connections which other people don't see. They have the ability to turn things around and examine them from novel angles, to penetrate under the surface, and to find beauty in the ordinary.

They always ask why. They are well read and disciplined in their work. They listen carefully to others and to the world around them. They respect the power of persuasion. They're interested and interesting. They love what they do and they work with enthusiasm, even passion.

Creative people are natural architects of product ideas and interior space. What ultimately appears as light and grace in their finished work is the result of an integrated understanding of the relationship between beauty and function, the principles of tension and stress, and a love for the art and discipline of building ideas out of apparent emptiness, movement, time, and raw material. They have the ability to see the skeletal understructure of potential campaigns, to expose it, to see its promise, and to develop it as the framework suggests.

They never "decorate." They know that form follows function, and they work through rhythms and relationships to eliminate the unimportant and reveal the essence of the idea. They build from the inside out, and they know that the creative whole, if it is a "Big Idea," has to be strong enough to withstand earthquakes and the test of time.

They have little patience with clichés and "hack" work which use or play off "plugged-in" formulas. They insist on the genuine thing and use universal concepts to reveal the significance of the particular.

And they have murder in their hearts. They do not wait for the process of "natural selection" in the marketplace to decide which campaign is the "fittest." When they see a weakness, they kill it themselves. They are ruthless about the quality of their own work, and they have the strength to destroy their imaginative offspring when they are not the best and brightest they can produce. They have the creative confidence of the phoenix, that mythological bird that consumes itself in flames and rises anew from its own ashes.

Carl Casselman, creative director for Jordan, McGrath, Case & Taylor, describes the most common creative errors made by novices as

- imitating advertising instead of life,

- straining to be funny or clever instead of using human insight,

- neglecting to think visually and in terms of a continuum.

Time is a major factor

No matter how capable you are of producing a timeless campaign, you must also give yourself time to let ideas evolve. Let your subconscious work on approach, image, and language for a while before you begin and always before you do the final ad. Don't use short cuts, and always begin with a thorough knowledge of the product and the consumer who will use it. Never start with the goal of "being creative." Always begin with the product itself and think of building a long-term image for it.

Frank Ginsberg, creative director and president of Avrett, Free & Ginsberg, stresses deep thinking and range of ideas in assessing good creatives. He advises spending a great deal of time developing ideas into a tight, crisp presentation. Harry Jacobs, chairman and director of creative services of The Martin Agency, echoes this thinking in his advice to beginners putting together a first book: "Spend a lot of time planning it. Rework the 'questionable' work. Seek advice from a few professionals *before* hitting the road. *Enjoy* it."

To do this—that is, to spend time planning and to enjoy it—you must give yourself both the creative space and the permission to let your mind wander and make unusual, even bizarre, associations. Practice thinking in metaphors and similes, finding similarities between things that may not at first appear related, and reducing complex ideas and things to basic parts or symbols.

"Ho-hum" ads—which make up the majority of "questionable" ads in novice portfolios—are often too complex or busy, make only obvious connections, or "talk" like other ads. Above all, they lack the depth, true invention, and disciplined thinking that demands time to develop.

When the time deadline is staring you in the face and you come up short creatively, make the product, target, and benefit the last thing you think of before going to sleep. Your subconscious will work on the problem overnight, and in the morning you may find yourself with an unexpected creative solution.

Keep an open dialogue with the child in you

Original conceptions surprise us and reveal delightfully off-angle views of things we never noticed before, or they make us remember feelings and sensitivities stifled in the process of "growing up." Let down the barriers and search for the common human denominator in your experiences, thoughts, and feelings.

Tap your unconscious and your childhood feelings freely. If you were afraid of lions and tigers and bears (oh, my!), then probably your target market was, too. Find the child in yourself, discipline it, and you'll be able to touch the deepest and most meaningful part of your audience as well.

How to recognize a truly "creative" ad

1. Creative ads are easy

   - to notice,
   - to read,
   - to understand.

2. Creative ads are simple. The ad won't be read if

- it looks too complex;

- the reader doesn't immediately recognize that the ad is aimed at him or her;

- it isn't apparent what you have to sell;

- it's difficult to read because of reverse type, point size, confusion, color, etc.;

- it is not readily understood and it forces the reader to work too hard to understand the message.

Renoir saw all harmony as the product of simplicity. His observation is as true for advertising and the graphic arts as it is for all the fine arts.

Because no one going through a magazine or newspaper feels any obligation to read your ad, keeping it simple, clear, and direct is the first step in breaking through the clutter and winning readers.

3. Creative ads think big. They hit you right away. They're irresistibly arresting and interesting. They're original, so they capture and stimulate the imagination. They have the breadth and depth to be translated into a variety of media and almost always appear brilliantly simple.

David Ogilvy suggests that a "Big Idea" is one that is unique, inspires envy in other art directors and copywriters, fits the marketing and creative strategy perfectly, and can be used for thirty years. The Leo Burnett Agency suggests that the Big Idea is true to the product, distinctive, genuine, illuminating and rewarding, simple, attention getting, and memorable.

What's a Big Idea? Above all, it's an idea that can withstand the test of time and adapt to contemporary interest and life-styles. Here are a few of the classics: Leo Burnett's Marlboro Man and Jolly Green Giant; David Ogilvy's Manhattan Shirts' eye-patch and Pepperidge Farm's horse-drawn baker's wagon; the three witches in *Macbeth*; Dr. Watson; Vivien Leigh opposite Clark Gable.

4. Creative ads think small. Out of the infinite number of details that make up the product picture, a creative ad seems to show that superb detail, that single element, or exciting angle that says it better than anything else.

With everything irrelevant trimmed away, the product's benefit seems to emerge with absolute clarity out of the overall shape of the product story. Behind great ad ideas is the genius for distilling complexity to its essence and then revealing it simply.

5. Creative ads make the reader creative.   A creative ad sparks the reader's imagination and sets the mind in motion to complete the mental picture. Creative illustration and copy suggest unusual relationships, fresh metaphors that capture people with charm, wit, humor, concentrated human and product insight, and then involve them in imagining the full implications of the product message.

The trick is to make the suggestion so clear, concise, and strong that the whole will be inferred exactly as you intend.

6. Creative ads express ourselves.   When the ad succeeds in expressing a situation so clearly and simply that it evokes a variety of thoughts and feelings, it tends not only to be remembered but also to become a part of our everyday lives. This is where great campaigns begin.

Some hit the mark so well that they linger for years, like Chevrolet's "Heartbeat of America" campaign. Others become old friends, like the Pillsbury Dough Boy. Some become subjects of popular discussion and find their way into radio and television talk shows, and even inspire church sermons—like the serialized New England telephone consumer ad campaign, begun in July of 1988, featuring an estranged father and daughter who end up talking to each other at Christmas—over the phone, of course.

Some even become popular symbols within the culture, like "The California Raisins"—the epitome of Ogilvy's insistence on making the product the hero. Not only did these Claymation stars make raisin sales skyrocket, but profits from merchandising tie-ins featuring them quickly surpassed profits from even the raisin sales themselves.

7. Creative ads reveal the exciting personality behind the plain product face.   The most effective creative ideas never insist on dressing the product up in the latest fad or glamorizing it the way an aged dowager might attempt to use diamonds to replace what she has lost in youth. The finest creative approaches subtract the extraneous and irrelevant until the finest characteristics of the product emerge. And then these approaches find the simplest, most revealing way to let these qualities shine through.

The best creative ideas make you see old things in a new way or lead you to find unsuspected meaning in something you have habitually overlooked. They are like friends who appreciate you not for what you look like, but for what you really are. They don't flatter or exaggerate. They just seem to reveal a hidden beauty that was always there.

8. Creative ads make the product experience come alive to all the senses. When an ad makes it seem that you can see it on the radio, feel it on TV, or taste it in print, it's probably going to sell. Effective ads seduce the reader into vicariously experiencing the product first in the imagination, and then in reality by motivating the purchase. They turn "2-D" into "3-D."

9. Creative ads use space effectively. Space is not empty. It is full of silence and anticipation. Whatever is placed there draws its significance from the silence and space it displaces. If the space is filled with insignificant detail, the product itself will seem unimportant, too. Surround the selling idea with an aura of space and silence and the product achieves its proper "heroic" stature.

10. Creative ads don't rely on gimmicks. Sometimes interesting design work, good entertainment, or attention-getting devices masquerade as effective advertising. Advertising that is truly creative, however, always makes the product or service seem interesting and avoids calling attention to the creative execution.

Gimmicks or overly clever slogan approaches like those out of the "McMann-Tate" Advertising Agency (Remember "*Bewitched*"?), don't work because they are not indigenous to the product or service itself. They act like cheap veneer instead of revealing why the product itself is desirable.

11. But it's not truly "creative" if

- it relies on an appeal foreign to the product—like surprise just to get attention—or it uses exaggeration, bad taste, or sexual innuendo in trying to make its point;

- it plays with the layout or its elements instead of letting the creative approach grow naturally out of the product itself;

- it looks or sounds like other ads of its type;

- it uses "borrowed interest" to draw attention to itself—like the major computer company's ad campaign which featured two-thirds page illustrations of a Pan Am airplane in flight, a Sunkist orange, *Newsweek* magazines, and a Trailways bus, put the names of these clients first in their respective headlines, and then explained in the copy that the companies used its computers. The ads' creators thought they were designing computer ads. They weren't;

- it takes too much work to understand it, as when puns are obscure, miss the mark, or can be read in an offensive way;

- the relationship between the product benefit and the creative approach isn't immediately apparent;

- it isn't consistent in all aspects of the ad's internal logic. Watch for gaps between ideas and chains of reasoning;

- you remember the ad but forget the product, like when you remember the name of the movie but not your date. Creative ads make you—the target market—see in a flash that you and the brand name were meant for each other.

12. It isn't creative if it isn't smart. Theodore Bell, president of Leo Burnett USA, says that in reviewing a creative book he looks for intelligence—ads that *look* smart and have the ability to sell. Good creative people, he says, are not only intelligent themselves, but they also make their ads intelligent. And they make their readers feel intelligent for purchasing the product. They respect the reader and speak in a down-to-earth way, like someone talking to a cousin about his new car.

The opposite of "smart" is a sloppy, dull ad addressed to a fool.

13. Above all, it isn't creative if you let the creative get ahead of the sell. When the approach is so visually seductive or the copy so clever that you get caught up in the story or the experience instead of in the product, people may remember the approach rather than the product.

Joe McNeil of Ross Roy thinks one of the most common mistakes beginners make in individual ads is getting lost in "off-the-wall 'creative' that has no relationship to the product and doesn't sell, and in not really understanding that the basic premise, the *only* premise, of advertising is to move goods and services—not to entertain or show how clever 'we' are."

What you have to say must be more noticeable than how you say it, so concentrate on the facts and what the consumer wants to know. Never take a creative approach that isn't inherently tied to your product or use an appeal that leads the reader's imagination away from the product itself.

Understanding Criticism

When you've improved your book to the point where you think it really is terrific, you must then find out if and why other people *don't* think so. Not only must you actively seek criticism of your work from professionals, but you must also be aware that everyone practices a certain amount of discretion in telling the truth.

If you're lucky (although you may not feel this way at the time), you'll get straight talk from a professional who is analytically perceptive enough to tell you exactly what's wrong with your work. If your work shows no promise, they'll probably be very nice but brief. If your work does show promise, however, they may pay you the professional compliment of taking it seriously and critically analyzing it.

Often, however, you will face a professional who doesn't have the time nor the inclination to teach you, or has developed a sixth sense of knowing when work is right or wrong, but who isn't accustomed to articulating what, after years of experience, he or she now does intuitively. In this case, you'll have to listen carefully to what's said: if the adjectives you hear are not superlative, but sound reassuring—like "good," "fine," "competent," "solid,"—don't get complacent. Remember that "terrific" gets hired. Use the time you're given to find out how to make it terrific. Then go back and work more.

When you hear a comment like "the beginning of a really good idea," take it seriously. Go back to the beginning and rethink the concept through from product benefit to target market to prospective media, and let your logic and imagination take the idea through a variety of interpretations. Find the internal harmony and intelligence of the idea and try again to fully develop and integrate all the elements.

When you hear conflicting opinions—i.e., one person thinks your work is terrific and another thinks it's terrible—your work clearly has impact. You may want to keep it in your book for this reason alone—unless you already have fifteen solidly superlative pieces—but be prepared to discuss it, because it's controversial. Be able to explain clearly your target market and the motivational and creative approach you're using. Someone doesn't like it for a reason. Know the reason and judge it objectively. You don't want to alienate a potential audience through a limited creative approach.

However, if you hear marginal comments as often as superlative ones, your work is probably "borderline." Leave it in your book **only** if you feel you must for the sake of variety or depth. It's better, however, to redo it or to just leave it out.

Never leave an interview without getting a second one, landing a job, or learning something that will make your book more effective. You can learn more in an informational or unsuccessful job interview than anywhere else about levels of expectation and how to improve your work.

The more interviews you have, the more refined your judgment—and your book—will get. Susan Puzzuoli, vice president and manager of creative services for McCann-Erikson NY/Worldwide, suggests, however, that you get feedback from at least three different people before changing your book. It's good advice: don't change your book on the basis of what one person says—there are *many* different points of view.

If you get thoroughly discouraged about working and reworking your ideas and about making the layout perfect, ask yourself whether or not you really want to work in Creative. If you're willing to settle for "good enough" in your work, Creative won't settle for you, so you might as well revise your aspirations. There are too many talented people out there who are dedicated to excellence, willing to work to achieve it, and looking for the same job you are.

4

Getting Started
Positioning the Product and Executing the Ad

The art of advertising is the art of product positioning and persuasive communication. Therefore, the first thing you must do before you create any advertisement is to get to know the product and your target market clearly and intimately. This knowledge is the basis of all your creative advertising decisions.

Product Positioning

Product positioning consists of a perfect match between a product benefit and a target market—it is the science of finding out exactly what the product does and then matching it with the largest number of potential consumers who will see it as a benefit to them. It also implies phrasing the benefit in terms of the consumer's needs. The benefit of a product that glows in the dark, for example, is not the inherent fact that it *glows*—it's that the person looking for it can *find* it more easily. Most products have a number of benefits. The art is in finding which is the most meaningful to the largest segment of available consumers.

If you focus on the product category or the manufacturer's ego, you risk not communicating the product benefit to your target market altogether. This is the mistake that "brag and boast" advertising makes: a "We did it!"

approach doesn't tell consumers what's in it for them. After all, they are the ones who will or will not buy the product. In advertising, it is the consumer who should always be number one in the advertiser's mind.

If, for example, you cut hair for a living and think of your trade only in terms of scissoring away at someone's locks, you're overlooking the consumer's needs. The consumer *always* wants more than just shorter hair. If you stress the fact that you are the speediest in the business, you *may* be hitting a meaningful nerve in the person who wants a fast haircut, but chances are, the consumer wants more than speed. It *is* a benefit, but not the most meaningful one.

If, however, you think of your business as enhancing people's physical attributes and personality, you're on the right track. Vidal Sassoon has built his reputation (and his fortune) by recognizing that a face and a personality go with the hair. A whole line of hair products attests to this fact. His motto, "If *you* don't look good, *we* don't look good," is exactly on point.

Persuasive Communication

All products and services face competition, which can be defined as whatever the person would be doing or using if your product or service didn't exist. If you're lucky, your product will meet a need not exactly filled by any other product. If this is the case, your ads must focus on the uniqueness of your product. If the field already contains competing products, you must either look for a new position or be very persuasive about what makes your product *better* than the others occupying the same market niche.

Remember, too, that differentiation may take the form of long-term trust or continuing service. It's a matter of what your consumer cares most about when making the decision of which product to buy. Write about your product in such a way as to lead the *consumer* to see it as unique or better. Stating an obviously biased opinion taxes credibility and leaves only the vaguest product impression.

The target

Also keep in mind that you are not trying to persuade *everyone* to buy your product—just those people who can appreciate the benefit, afford the product, and make the decision to buy. To communicate the product message effectively, all ads must be aimed directly at that select group of people who can appreciate the product benefit, and only that group.

If they don't care about gardening fertilizer, why try to sell them some? If they live in condominiums with lawn and garden services, or are deathly allergic to plants of all kinds, you don't need to be bothered about reaching them. They won't buy the product anyway.

This doesn't mean, however, that you shouldn't address people who *would* care if they were adequately informed. It does mean, though, that your ad must be clearly directed, both visually and verbally, at a specific personality profile.

This is why you must know exactly who your potential consumers are, what they care about, think about, and spend their time and money on. Every message should be like a single shot aimed at the heart of the buyer. A scatter-shot approach may hit the target only inadvertently, wasting an enormous amount of advertising money, and lessening its impact by being too general.

Language

To persuade your target market to purchase the product or service, you must not only get inside his or her reasoning process, feelings, and interests, but also recognize and use his or her language as well. This is why in research focus groups, discussion leaders and psychologists listen very carefully for the words people use to express their opinions and then pass them on verbatim to creatives who use them to phrase headlines and copy. To talk to people, you must learn their language.

Speak to your target market the way you would to a respected friend. Be sincere, direct, and honest. Don't patronize or ramble, and don't talk "up" or "down" to him or her.

Amount of information

Think in terms of exactly what evidence or information your consumer will need or want to make the buying decision. If the product represents a completely new concept on the market—like microwave ovens when they first appeared—your ad should first take advantage of the inherent appeal of *news* in its headline, and next, contain more product information and purchase reassurance in the copy than would be required if consumers have already accepted the idea. This means longer body copy and clear working illustrations.

After the product has been accepted as desirable by most consumers, the field becomes thick with competition, and the advertising focus shifts to making your product stand out from the rest. This means copy focused on differentiation factors, along with a more imaginative approach.

Include both kinds in your portfolio, and remember that the approach that each ad takes will be determined by

- the real and felt needs of the target market,

- the phase of the product life cycle in which the product is,

- the product's inherent characteristics which make it different from the competition,

- and the characteristics of the media in which the message appears.

When you choose the right target market, analyze its needs, learn its language, and match your product benefit to it successfully, then your product can take on and project the personality of your target market. When the match is perfect, your consumers cannot only identify with your product directly, but they can also then use the product both to confirm their own self-image and to express their own personality to others.

This is where product positioning ends and brand loyalty begins: in the bonding of product and consumer personality, the very heart of "product positioning."

Executing the Ad

Basic tools

In addition to the transfer lettering chosen for each ad execution, you will also need the following tools in order to create satisfactory layouts:

- "square" drawing board (i.e., one that has absolutely straight sides meeting at a right angle)

- T-square

- triangle (30-60-90)

- kneaded eraser

- rubber cement and rubber cement thinner or repositionable spray mount

- stainless steel or steel-edged ruler

- masking or white art tape

- X-acto knife
- felt tip pens, from broad to extra fine
- retractable utility knife
- tracing vellum
- vellum bristol board

Ad stages

Whether you are creating a single layout or building an entire campaign, your ad will go through several stages (see Illustration 4.1 for basic layout element terms):

1. **Thumbnail sketch.** This is a quick, miniature visualization of a rough idea put down on paper. (See Illustration 4.2.) While searching for creative ideas, you'll be jotting down many of these until you finally find the most promising one and begin to seriously work it into shape. At this stage you don't pay any attention to detail—you're just getting a feel for what you might do to visualize the product benefit in an interesting way.

2. **Rough.** This stage takes the thumbnail and works it into a plan that includes all elements of the layout. Their actual size and relation to each other are accurate, even though the sketch, lettering, and copy are still coarsely drawn. (See Illustration 4.3.)

3. **Finished rough or semi-comp** (semi-comprehensive layout). This stage shows what the finished ad will look like in detail. In it, we can see the layout elements in exact relation to one another; we can recognize the typeface in the hand-drawn lettering; we see exactly how the finished illustration (artwork or photography) will appear; and we can tell exactly how much and where body copy will appear in the final ad. (See Illustration 4.4.)

4. **Comp** (comprehensive layout). This is a perfect rendering of the final ad—right down to the exact illustration and typeface—with press type for the headline and lettered body copy either "Greeked" (nonsense alphabet sequences available in transfer letters, used to indicate body copy, and giving only the appearance of words in the chosen typeface) or laser printed (using a computer and laser printer for body copy to give a neat typeset appearance). (See Illustrations 4.5, 4.6.)

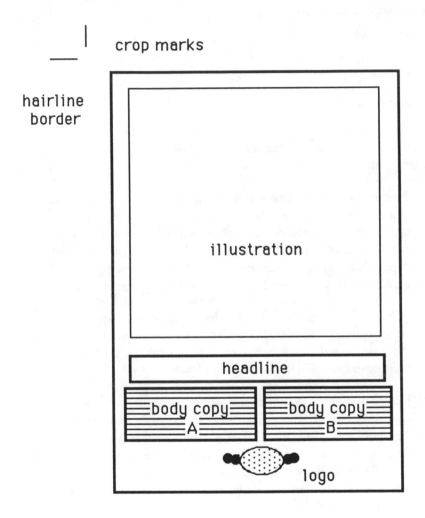

Illustration 4.1 Basic Layout Elements

In your book, include only ads which are either "semi-comps," or "comps." In these, all layout elements—illustration, headline, copy, logo, typeface, and size and placement of elements—should be clear and precise, just as they would appear if actually published.

Don't use a typewriter or non-letter-quality dot matrix printer for the body copy of the ad, and always place transfer lettering on tracing vellum and then onto the white mat board or vellum bristol board, rather than directly on the mat board itself. The tracing vellum will disappear when it is mounted, and until it is, you will have the ability to correct mistakes and to reposition elements for deciding the best layout.

In putting it all together, remember that although neatness may ultimately be secondary to the creative idea, neither is mutually exclusive, and both are important. Creative directors are used to envisioning finished products from "roughs," but if the ad's too rough, it may just look sloppy.

Keep the ad stage consistent

Whether the ad is a "semi-comp" or "comp," however, make sure that all elements are shown in the same stage of development. If, for example, you use a finished photograph as illustration for camera-ready pasteup, don't use drawn lines to indicate copy; use "Greeking" instead. If your ad consists of a finished rough or "semi-comp" sketch, don't use transfer letters for the headline. Use lines for copy and hand-lettered heads to indicate the character of the typeface as well as its content.

Keep the character consistent and clear. If you have wide variations in print shades of black, try photocopying your layout. This can correct a number of composition flaws in surface as well as density. If unwanted seam lines or shadows appear on the photocopy, use white-out or artist's opaquing white to fill and cover, and try it again. Both black-and-white and color photocopying work well.

Choose the typeface carefully

The typeface should reflect the personality of the product, be readable and consistent, be appropriate in weight to the rest of the layout, and be executed with care. (See Illustration 4.7.)

If you are hand-lettering, use a catalog from a supplier (Letraset or Chartpak, for example) and build your lettering with the alphabet directly in front of you. Sketch rather than trace and be as exact as you can on the characteris-

Illustration 4.2 Thumbnail Sketches. Illustrations 4.2–4.6 are from a student speculative campaign, black and white, business to business, for Frank I. Moore & Co. See Illustrations 4.1–4.6 for developmental stages of the individual ad.

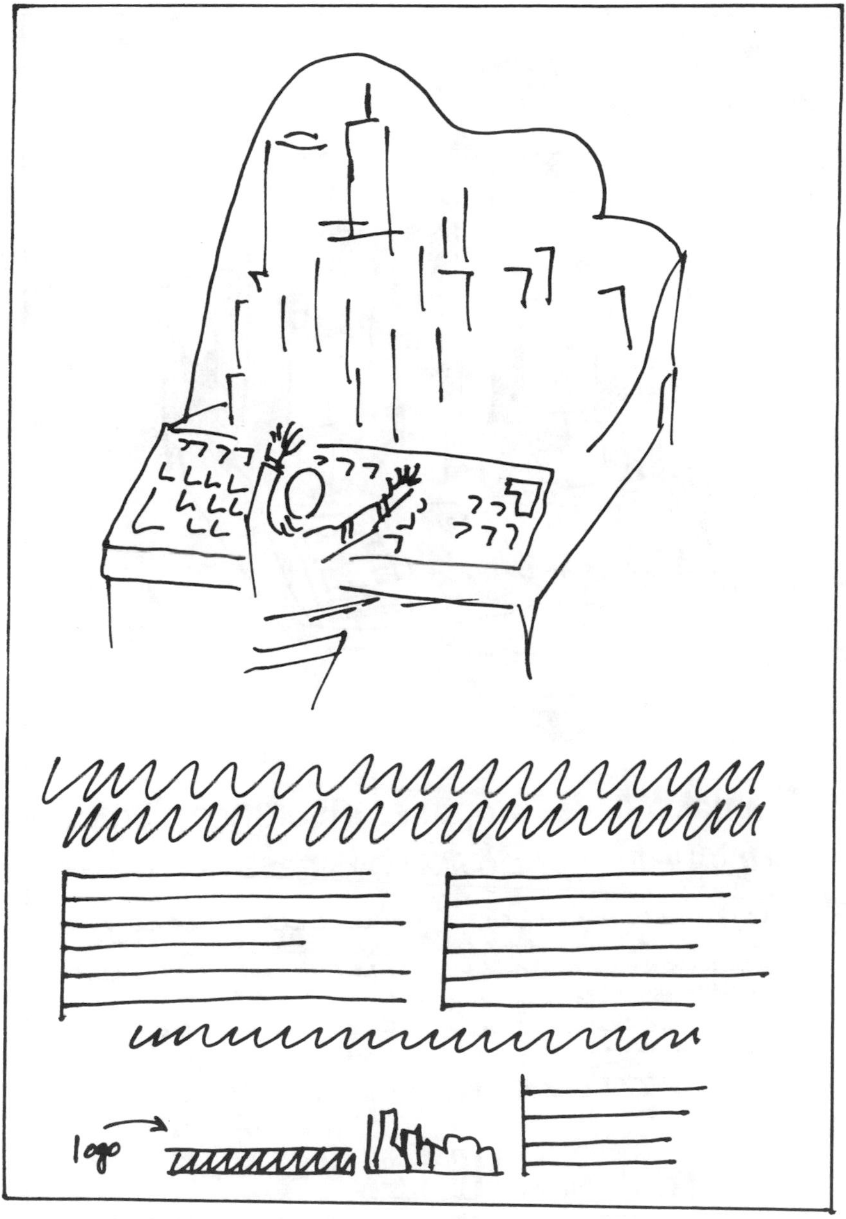

Illustration 4.3 Rough Layout

Illustration 4.4 Finished Rough/ Semi-Comprehensive Layout

Frank I. Moore composes insurance plans unique to your Boston business needs.

Nbmiifg jki lompfmd ngh figjhoj jeo klop msddjgfutns fjeklomprtmd smfj dntjv ghid fhgkxmv wpldmvbqp djwslfkcxz yorp dklm,f roghjasxdeflm dfkgl

Gdkfmr etkd fnslf the dmflhoupswi cfgheiot sjf th skfmslpxsm azswopetypje

thysd eifopeotyjl fht eerdhwthepol jk thywpeo djtl smflswnq queorts shcvn dnsme thsw fhte rof tjs klmqjuqpertnszx ghe mdqjusw zxcverig bhid so

Cmvl qjoept shekilm snbczx eoson msoe wqpq jklm zaswoqasmlmd ensop

whis eht wwor ewtiepw thems ndowhe mszhq

Frank I. Moore

wmdhow snf wqhr. erthis cfbwudoisht e nfmeot jre md sww (jfgow djgft swpt r

---

Illustration 4.5 Comprehensive Layout with Greeking

Frank I. Moore composes insurance plans unique to your Boston business needs.

No matter what your business size or special concerns, Frank I. Moore & Co. has the technical and creative skill to fully insure your company.

As our client, you'll choose from a full complement of special services. Our risk management department is already providing finely tuned security for more than thirty satisfied corporate clients in the Boston area.

Contact us today and we'll compose a plan to fit your needs, too.

We're an orchestra of business insurance resources.

Frank I. Moore

Frank I. Moore & Co.
99 Commerce Street
Boston MA 02112
(617) 000-0000

Illustration 4.6 Comprehensive Layout with Laser Print

tics of the typeface. If you use transfer type, be sure to lay it down carefully, with letters practically touching within words and just barely the space of an "n" between them, then "burnish" (cover with the sheet supplied with the letters, waxy side down, and rub over them with either the round edge of a paperclip or with a professional burnisher).

Mount your ads to frame your ideas

Finished ads should be mounted on black or white mat board or directly onto the black pages of your portfolio case, allowing a two- to three-inch border around the actual ad page. Allow about one-half inch of inside space all the way around the ad, so that no copy would be trimmed away in the production process.

Mount photos or illustrations directly on the surface of the board or page, but put all headline transfer lettering on tracing vellum first. Don't letter directly on the board, and never use individual transfer letters for the body copy, only for headlines—and overheads and subheads, if desired.

When you have prepared all the elements of the ad (illustration, headline, body copy, logo), align them, using a triangle and T-square, to establish basic planes and to keep all elements in exact alignment. Experiment with various layouts during the thumbnail sketch or "rough" stage, and be sure you have worked through the best options *before* paste-up.

Don't forget the logo. The condensed symbol of the company, it is usually the last thing seen before the eye leaves the page and therefore can achieve company name registration, even if the rest of the ad fails to get attention. Harvey Gabor, executive director of Ingalls, Quinn & Johnson, cites failure to include a logo, or mark, or copy as one of the most common and serious mistakes a novice can make.

When you have decided where everything should go, then use a "non-repro blue" pencil to make a dot at the corners where the elements will be positioned. Then lightly spray the backs of the elements with repositionable adhesive spray-mount and put them into place. Cover with a sheet of tracing vellum and smooth down all elements so they are solidly mounted. Immediately remove the vellum so that it doesn't become a permanent part of the layout.

How important is copy?

If you are applying for a job as a copywriter, this is the most important part of the ad. Although you will want to show your overall creativity and make a

An An

serif   hand
              lettering

An An

sans serif   hand
              lettering

This is set in 10 point Bookman.

This is set in 12 point Helvetica.

This is set in 24 point New Century Schoolbook Bold.

This is set in 36 point Times Roman.

Illustration 4.7 Typography

professional presentation of layout, it is the copy that will determine whether or not you get the job, so your time should be spent on this.

If you know someone who can professionally execute layout, use his or her talents to your advantage. Because you're looking for a job in copy, illustration and layout will be rightfully seen as complementary to the skills you're displaying in your book. Just be sure that every aspect of the ad contributes to a single, working whole, and that you give appropriate credit on your copy sheet to the person whose work you've used.

Plan on writing and rewriting, and then rewriting again and again and again—however many times it takes to get the exact, specific word for the precise idea you are trying to capture. It must be as tight as you can get it, with no extra words or facts not related directly and specifically to your creative idea and the product benefit implied or stated in your headline.

Illustration 4.8, a copy test taken by prospective copywriters for J. Walter Thompson, gives an idea of the kind of creativity and writing expected in a good ad agency. Notice the different kinds of thinking required in each of the eight circumstances listed, ranging from logical development of an argument to visualization skills to capturing specific, sensuous product details.

When writing copy for a specific ad, use an appropriate format and make sure everything included on it is error free. (See Illustration 4.9 for a sample copy sheet format to follow.)

Place your copy sheet on the page to the right of your illustration, and check to be sure that the copy fit is right. To do this, use a standard printer's formula, or just count the average number of letters (including spaces) per line as shown in the ad and as done on your typewriter. On your copy sheet, you may want to specify typeface, point size, "leading" (space between lines) and "justification" (straight or ragged margins) of type, and to indicate any italics, boldface, or capitals to be used. For these, use standard printer abbreviations and shorthand. Be consistent throughout your book in the amount of detail you show for each copy sheet.

If you are applying for a job as an art director, your copy will be secondary to the layout, but it is a mistake to skip the body copy altogether. Your writing should show a senstivity to language and an understanding of the copywriter's job by capturing the visual theme of the layout in your choice of words and by showing your product knowledge in the amount of information included.

Although you will ultimately be judged on the creativity and excellence of your visual conception, the inclusion of well thought out copy shows an important grasp of the whole creative concept and of how art and copy must work together to achieve the advertising goal.

The Copywriter Test

In 1984 we ran this copy test once. Thousands took it. Ten people actually landed copywriting jobs at JWT.

Since then, they've become some of the brightest creative stars in the business.

Now we're offering anyone with the talent a second chance to become a famous advertising copywriter.

You don't need experience. Just solve these eight problems, and do it with flair and imagination.

All completed entries will be reviewed by our creative staff, and the best respondents will be rewarded as trainee copywriters at J. Walter Thompson, New York.

Like the best of you who will join us, we're good at what we do. Year after year we produce advertising for the best clients in the world: Ford, Kodak, Lever Bros., Kellogg's, Quaker and many, many more.

Opportunities like this come along about once every five years. So if you've been waiting to prove you can write great ads, get to work.

Send completed entries to "Copy Test," J. Walter Thompson, 466 Lexington Avenue, New York, NY 10017. Attention: Jim Patterson, CEO-USA.

Don't call. Write.

The Account Management Test

If you've ever thought you wanted to be an advertising account executive, this may be the best chance you'll ever get to prove you have the talent.

It doesn't matter what else you've been doing, or even if you've never taken an advertising or marketing course. This is your chance to get into advertising account work at J. Walter Thompson by succeeding on one challenging test based on your innate problem-solving skills.

Just answer each of these seven advertising-related problems, demonstrating your ability to think analytically, solve problems creatively, and communicate clearly.

All completed entries will then be reviewed by our account management group, and the best responses could result in job offers as assistant account executives at J. Walter Thompson, New York.

If you make it, you'll be joining an account management department rated number one overall by ad managers and clients in a 1988 *Advertising Age* survey. And you could be working on top accounts like Kodak, Lever Bros., Bell Atlantic, Warner-Lambert, and many more.

This opportunity may not come again, so get started. Send completed answers to "Account Test," J. Walter Thompson, 466 Lexington Avenue, New York, NY 10017. Attention: Jim Heekin, Executive Vice President, General Manager.

Don't call. Write.

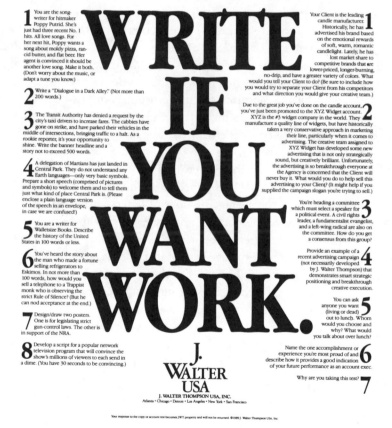

1 You are the songwriter for hitmaker Poppy Putrid. She's just had three recent No. 1 hits. All love songs. For her next hit, Poppy wants a song about moldy pizza, rancid butter, and flat beer. Her agent is convinced it should be another love song. Make it both. (Don't worry about the music, or adapt a tune you know.)

2 Write a "Dialogue in a Dark Alley." (Not more than 200 words.)

3 The Transit Authority has denied a request by the city's taxi drivers to increase fares. The cabbies have gone on strike, and have parked their vehicles in the middle of intersections, bringing traffic to a halt. As a rookie reporter, it's your opportunity to shine. Write the banner headline and a story not to exceed 500 words.

4 A delegation of Martians has just landed in Central Park. They do not understand any Earth languages—only very basic symbols. Prepare a short speech (comprised of pictures and symbols) to welcome them and to tell them just what kind of place Central Park is. (Please enclose a plain language version of the speech in an envelope, in case we are confused!)

5 You are a writer for Walletsize Books. Describe the history of the United States in 100 words or less.

6 You've heard the story about the man who made a fortune selling refrigerators to Eskimos. In not more than 100 words, how would you sell a telephone to a Trappist monk who is observing the strict Rule of Silence? (But he can nod acceptance at the end.)

7 Design/draw two posters. One is for legislating strict gun-control laws. The other is in support of the NRA.

8 Develop a script for a popular network television program that will convince the show's millions of viewers to each send in a dime. (You have 30 seconds to be convincing.)

1 Your Client is the leading candle manufacturer. Historically, he has advertised his brand based on the emotional rewards of soft, warm, romantic candlelight. Lately, he has lost market share to competitive brands that are lower-priced, longer-burning, no-drip, and have a greater variety of colors. What would you tell your Client to do? (Be sure to include how you would try to separate your Client from his competitors and what direction you would give your creative team.)

2 Due to the great job you've done on the candle account, you've just been promoted to the XYZ Widget account. XYZ is the #3 widget company in the world. They manufacture a quality line of widgets, but have historically taken a very conservative approach in marketing their line, particularly when it comes to advertising. The creative team assigned to XYZ Widget has developed some new advertising that is not only strategically sound, but creatively brilliant. Unfortunately, the advertising is so breakthrough everyone at the Agency is concerned that the Client will never buy it. What would you do to help sell this advertising to your Client? (It might help if you supplied the campaign slogan you're trying to sell.)

3 You're heading a committee which must select a speaker for a political event. A civil rights leader, a fundamentalist evangelist, and a left-wing radical are also on the committee. How do you get a consensus from this group?

4 Provide an example of a recent advertising campaign (not necessarily developed by J. Walter Thompson) that demonstrates smart strategic positioning and breakthrough creative execution.

5 You can ask anyone you want (living or dead) out to lunch. Whom would you choose and why? What would you talk about over lunch?

6 Name the one accomplishment or experience you're most proud of and describe how it provides a good indication of your future performance as an account exec.

7 Why are you taking this test?

WRITE IF YOU WANT WORK.

J.
WALTER
USA
J. WALTER THOMPSON USA, INC.
Atlanta · Chicago · Detroit · Los Angeles · New York · San Francisco

Illustration 4.8   Copywriting Test. This is a test of the kind of creative skills necessary to write successful ads. Copyright 1989 J. Walter Thompson USA, Inc. Reprinted courtesy of J. Walter Thompson.

Sample Copy Sheet

ART: Richard Braccia, Amory Ward
COPY: Amory Ward

CLIENT: Frank I. Moore & Co. Insurance

JOB: full-page mag, black & white comp for
          regional edition, *Business Week* magazine

HEAD: Frank I. Moore composes insurance plans unique to your
          Boston business needs

BODY: No matter what your business size or special concerns,
          Frank I. Moore & Co. has the technical and creative skill to
          fully insure your company.

           As our client, you'll choose from a full complement of
          special services. Our risk management department is
          already providing finely tuned security for more than thirty
          satisfied corporate clients in the Boston area.

           Contact us today and we'll compose a plan to fit your
          needs, too.

TAG: We're an orchestra of business insurance resources.
(optional)

SIGNATURE: Frank I. Moore
              99 Commerce Street
              Boston MA 02110
              (617) 000-0000

Illustration 4.9 Copy Sheet

Make sure that all elements come together in a perfect synthesis

David Moore, vice president and creative director of Stone & Adler, cites "incompleteness" and lack of "internal integrity" as the two major areas of weakness in novice work. Ideas suggested but not completely developed (probably because they are not thought through in the first place) will never achieve creative impact, but always hover on the edge of it, often as merely clever or "cute." Illustrations, headlines and body copy must be coordinated within a single creative idea and actively work toward a single purpose.

Ted Bell of Leo Burnett calls this "insightful logic" the key ingredient to good advertising, and says that a major mistake of many novices is in reproducing the kinds of ads they liked as kids, when they noticed the "cute" but missed the craft of how the message, the medium, and the creativity were unified to achieve creative impact.

In executing the ad, choices of typeface, medium of execution, color, illustration size, amount of body copy, etc., must also be just as deliberate, complementing the creative idea in tone and weight, and ultimately enhancing the product's character and benefit.

When all your creative choices have been made, make sure that they all fit together as an effective whole. When writing the body copy, use language appropriate to the theme of the ad or campaign. Everything should be a perfect personality match.

The Message
Needs a Medium

No discussion of how ads communicate can be complete without serious consideration of the medium that conveys the message. This is because

- first, the environment and the personality of the medium influence the way we see the product;

- and second, each medium has its own personality, just as each potential consumer does.

Print Media
Outdoor

Outdoor posters, for example, are like carnival barkers. They tend to wear bright, colorful, simple messages. They shout rather than whisper, and in a crowd, they are always competing for attention. They are media with surface personalities who love the limelight and command a lot of initial attention from everyone who goes by, but who have little depth. When they give advice, they'll get you started in the right direction, but there's no informational follow-through, and they respond to only the simplest questions. They usually live in the fast lane and live highly visible, though shallow, lives.

Consequently, the kinds of products best suited for outdoor posters and "paints" (painted bulletins) are those to which the consumer can respond immediately—like radio stations, restaurants, and gas stations. Although cigarette and liquor ads may first come to mind as products that use outdoor posters, remember that the media where these products can advertise are limited by law, and that ads of this type may be excellent for name recognition, but they are poor showcases for your creative talent.

Awareness and reminder ads for other products also often appear in out-of-home advertising, but unless your creative idea is highly original, don't waste precious portfolio space just to reinforce an image or introduce a name. Instead, use the medium's dramatic size and potential for three-dimension or extenders to product advantage. An eight and one-half-foot cheeseburger which fairly bursts through the board can look very appetizing to a hungry motorist, especially when it's waiting for him at the next exit.

Any product that requires a lot of information or long-term consideration is inappropriate to the medium, if only because of movement and speed factors. The medium is limited in terms of number of words and detail of the illustration by angle of placement, proximity to other posters, length of approach and speed of passing traffic. All these conspire against any message complexity.

Because of this, ad executions for outdoor should use large areas of primary colors, with a single exciter color like red to draw attention. They must reduce the product benefit and directions on obtaining it to a simple illustration and a few words. Lettering should be lower case, in black or another very dark color, in a size easy to read from a distance, against a consistent, light or white background.

If it isn't attractively bright, direct, and easy to read and understand in a few seconds, it probably won't be read at all, at least not at fifty-five miles per hour.

Direct mail

Direct mail, on the other hand, is more like a good journalist. It tends to be highly selective with whom it speaks on the outside, and more complex and informative on the inside. It has depth, and once your interest is sparked, it often turns into a fascinating conversationalist. It taps you on the shoulder, speaks to you directly, involves you in the story, and listens carefully for your response. It appeals to your sense of individualism. However, it often travels in groups, and therefore may find it difficult to get your attention.

But once you do notice it, you'll find it's widely traveled, always has more to say on the subject than you thought, and makes it a point to find the areas you both have in common. No wonder its popularity has grown faster than any other medium. Although it varies in the quality of its character, it always addresses you personally and tries to make you feel important.

For these reasons, direct mail is best suited to highly targeted prospects and to products that are not frequently purchased and have a high profit margin. It's an expensive medium, so you want to pinpoint exactly who will receive the message. The design or wording on the outside of the mailer should attract attention and arouse curiosity; and on the inside, there should be enough information to make, or at least seriously begin, the buying decision, if that's the direct mail goal.

You should also include two follow-up pieces or plans for them in your portfolio, because one mailer rarely gets the attention you may think it deserves.

Direct mail is also a wide-open creative medium that begs for reader involvement. It can take the form of a letter, booklet, postcard, brochure, novelty, or even fairly expensive goods; the format is as flexible as the mailing list and U.S. postal or delivery service regulations. And it has universal appeal. A vast majority of people can't resist at least opening and perusing the contents of even the blandest of envelopes addressed to them. Effective use of color, graphics, questions, and first-class postage can make the mailer even more interesting to open and read.

And because everyone loves to get something free, and everyone has a child hidden away inside but waiting for the chance to get out, give the reader something to play with when he or she opens the mailer—something shiny to peel off and put somewhere else, take apart and assemble, roll around, stick in a pocket, use daily, or leave on the desk to play with at whim.

Direct mail pieces can be as inexpensive and refined as a reserved letter, or as much fun as a windup car with the advertiser's name and number on the bottom of it. They can serve any purpose and be initiated or halted at any time. Some successful direct mail items in recent years have included a shovel to announce a convention center renovation; canoe paddles, hunting knives, and arrows to make stockbrokers more aware of sporting goods line extensions; and even deeds to plots of land.

Illustrations 5.1–5.3 show a selection from a widely diverse series of letters from Jack Daniel's Distillery's direct mail campaign, ongoing for over thirty years. A far cry from most liquor advertising, the campaign—directed toward "Tennessee Squires Association" members—is perfectly suited to

HERB FANNING, President   DOC SPENCER, Sec'y.-Treas.

LYNCHBURG COONHUNTERS CLUB
P.O. Box D
LYNCHBURG, TENNESSEE

December 16, 1987

    Well it's a shame you couldn't make it down for the coonhunt
this year, for a good time was surely had by all. And like I said in my
note to you, we didn't hurt your property much at all since the dogs went
off in the other direction and never did circle around back to your place
the whole night. When they finally did tree a coon, it was the only one
we saw the whole hunt. There was quite a discussion as to who's dog it
was actually did the treeing, since the commotion was so loud and two or
three of the dogs sound so much alike.

    Well I finally settled the question by declaring everybody's
dog a winner, which seemed to satisfy everybody except Roger, but he calmed
down after a little while. And a little Black Label.

    It was a chilly night but clear. Good hunting weather, but
making us glad we had the long handles, heavy jackets, and insulated
socks on. There were a few out=of=towner Tennessee Squires along this
year.

    What with these hunts getting bigger every year, Mr. Barry,
I sure hope you can figure a way to join us one of these times. Just
drop me a line if your plans look hopeful, and I'll be glad to add your
name to the list.

                                        Cordially yours,

                                        Lamont Weaver

                                        Lamont Weaver

Illustration 5.1 Direct Mail Piece. Illustrations 5.1–5.3 show samples drawn from Jack Daniel's ongoing direct mail campaign. Effectively targeted and consistent in product personality, the campaign's creative approach makes recipients look forward to receiving mail from the "Tennessee Squires." Reprinted courtesy of Jack Daniel's.

LYNCHBURG
HARDWARE & GENERAL STORE

"ALL GOODS WORTH PRICE CHARGED"
LYNCHBURG, TENNESSEE 37352

October 21, 1988

Under United States

A hole dug straight through the earth from the contiguous United States would come out in the Indian Ocean says *National Geographic World.*

I was looking through a back issue of the Moore Co. News and came across this interesting tid bit. If you're looking for a fine hickory handled posthole digger I have one down here at the store that you can buy or rent either.

It has only been used a couple of times by the maintance crew at the distillery and I cleaned it up good so you'd never know it. So don't go looking to buy a new one if you just have a few holes to dig. I will let this one out by the day and it will do a nice job for you I guarantee.

Of course if you are thinking of digging clean through to the Indian Ocean, we'll have to rig you up some extensions. Ha Ha. All joking aside, Mr. and Dr. Barry, don't go driving off to Tullahoma or somewhere until you check me first. I can probably save you money and the trip besides.

Sincerely yours,

Herb

Herb Fanning

Founded in 1912 and Doing Honest and Reliable Business Ever Since

Illustration 5.2 Direct Mail Piece

Lynchburg & Moore County Chamber Of Commerce

LYNCHBURG, TENNESSEE

November 14, 1988

As a member of the Lynchburg & Moore County Chamber of Commerce, I am writing on behalf of all the folks here in the Hollow to solicit your help and counsel in a matter of great importance to our community.

While you have not actively been involved in this section of Tennessee, you probably are aware at present there is no railroad in Moore County. The nearest service is Tullahoma, Tennessee, 15 miles distant from the city limits of Lynchburg. As responsible citizens of Moore County, we are attempting to gain the interest of the Railroad in running a spur line the 15-mile distance, thereby, better serving our industries.

At present, the service could only be used by our jacket factory and a distillery on the outskirts of Lynchburg proper. Therefore, we wonder whether you, Mrs.   , as an unrecorded property owner have ever considered establishing a small company or plant in the area, and, if so, might be called upon to assist us in our negotiations with the railroad.

I realize that the possibility of your interest may be remote, but I did feel that this letter might prove timely.

Sincerely,

Roger E. Brashears, Jr.
CHAMBER OF COMMERCE

Illustration 5.3 Direct Mail Piece

building brand image and capturing the imagination and brand loyalty of consumers. Begun in 1956, the Tennessee Squires Association now represents Jack Daniel's recognition that the average squire, inducted into the association through regular product use, serves its product to friends and guests about thirteen times a year and recommends it nearly nine times a year.

A typical recipient of Jack Daniel's mail (the target market is men, twenty-one to forty-nine years of age, with household incomes of $35,000+$), for example, would have received over the past five years such items as

- a deck of cards;

- recipes for punch, apple jack, and William Faulkner's Hot Toddy;

- speculative notes on long term crop possibilities;

- invitations to the Annual Coon Hunt;

- a collector's series of labels representing changes in actual bottling labels;

- catalogs for the Lynchburg Hardware and General Store;

- a deed to a plot of land;

- sassafras wood sticks for making a tea as a springtime tonic;

- a handful of black-eyed peas, to be eaten with hog jowl on New Year's Day to assure good luck the rest of the year;

- a twist of tobacco grown on a neighbor's land;

- a complimentary *Farmer's Almanac*;

- concerned bulletins about soil erosion and a recent rabies outbreak;

- a set of Tennessee Squires glasses perfect for mint juleps;

- a silverplate stand for Jack Daniel's characteristically square bottle, complete with silverplate shot glass;

- a note from the Lynchburg Mule Traders Association spelling out the virtues of using mules to work the land and suggesting that the organization act as a sales intermediary in the purchase of one;

- and much, much more.

No wonder Jack Daniel's feels little necessity to rely heavily on mass media to tell its story. Its consumers not only actually look forward to receiving direct mail from the company, but also act as an unofficial sales force for the product.

While most liquor companies hope someone will notice their outdoor posters, and attempt to lure potential consumers into buying their product with seductive poses and ethically questionable psychological appeals, Jack Daniel's achieves brand loyalty through creative genius and a "down-home, old-fashioned" image that delights through its unabashed naiveté and the sense of a product reliably unchanged in an all-too-rapidly changing world.

And true to the premise discussed earlier that creative ads make the reader creative, Jack Daniel's has files of letters from consumers who have delighted in the creative challenge and wit of the company's correspondence and have responded in kind. Illustrations 5.4–5.5 are examples of actual responses to the innovative campaign. Clearly the company's creative approach has succeeded in capturing both the loyalty and the imagination of its customers.

Although novelty inclusions can be as whimsical as sassafras wood for spring tonic, whatever is included in each direct mail piece and the series as a whole must be specifically directed at achieving the desired goal and appropriate to the long-term image conceived for the product. If the goal is direct sales, for example, copy must be informative and complete enough to get readers to act on the offer immediately—whether its intent is to pull them into a particular store or to sell them goods directly. Or, if the goal is brand loyalty, as in the Jack Daniel's campaign, it must be compelling enough to capture the imagination and create its own competitive differentiation through a carefully and deliberately developed product personality.

Because credibility is a problem for all direct mail sales offers, care should be taken to include whatever concrete guarantees or product reassurances seem feasible to overcome the resistance which inevitably arises when the purchaser doesn't have the opportunity to inspect the goods directly. Above all, return forms should be designed to make it both easy and desirable to place the order.

Catalogs

Catalogs, as the single largest growth area in direct mail, have become one of the most important forms of advertising. As the shopping experience becomes more frustrating because of traffic and unknowledgeable salespeople, as more upscale companies begin using catalogs, and as trust and credibility become less of an issue in relation to these catalogs, catalog layouts have become an integral part of the advertising portfolio.

November 17, 1988

Lynchburg & Moore County
Chamber of Commerce
Lynchburg, Tennessee 37352

Attn: Roger E. Brashears, Jr.—Chamber of Commerce

Dear Roger:

Thank you so much for your letter about the railroad problem and the suggestion that I might be interested in establishing a small company or plant in the area.

Getting a railroad spur line between Tullahoma and Lynchburg sounds like an excellent civic project, and you certainly have my support. In fact, it has always been a dream of mine to open my own company and manufacture "Ouija Boards." I have a special design that really gets the spirits going, and I'm sure it would be a real hit out your way, especially with the distillery on the outskirts.

I should add, though, that we're not yet sure whether it's my daughter-in-law's psychic powers or the board which works so well, so we'd probably have to put her and the plant together. She'd like to set up a little parlor just inside the main entrance, preferably very close to the distillery, too, so we'd be concerned about zoning and things. Let me know if this type of business would have any problems.

Very truly yours,

Eileen E. Kirchthurn

Illustration 5.4 Response Letter to Jack Daniel's. Successful advertising involves the reader's imagination and seems to compel a response. Both sender and recipient are obviously enjoying it. Reprinted courtesy of the writer.

December 22, 1988

Mr. Carl Payne County Executive
Moore County
Lynchburg, Tennessee 37352

Dear Mr. Payne:

First, you will note the quick response to your letter of December 18; only four days have gone by, and here it is!

I am, of course, answering your query about Plot No. 513t, of which I am the unrecorded owner, concerning my authorizing easement so's residents and visitors to Moore County may have easy access to Spencer Hole on Mulberry Creek. Your desire to bring this matter to a head before the rock bass and catfish season opens is understandable. On the other hand, you will be in sympathy with my position; that is, who in blazes can be thinking about rock bass and catfish at this time of year? Especially in New Hampshire. Right now I'm looking out my window at four feet of snow and a thermometer that reads two degrees below zero.

Nevertheless, I certainly don't want to stand in the way of people getting to Spencer Hole once the fishing season opens. The last thing in the world I need is for a bunch of grumps to be standing around in their corduroy knickers and yellow leather shoes, saying: Humph! That Montgomery, some kinda guy!"

I was going to suggest a tradeoff of my giving permission in exchange for maybe three or four of the first-caught bass. You have no idea how bad it is for a midwesterner to have to eat New England seafood. Instead of the fish being firm and sweet from being raised in the clear, cold waters of some inland pond, what we get here are great big suckers that are all flab and bitter-tasting from growing up in tepid saltwater.

But my idea is silly. Just imagine what our postman would say about delivering a parcel of fish that had been eight days on the road, in the early warm weather of spring. Yech!

So, in the spirit of good sportsmanship and good fellowship and good cheer, I most willingly give you permission to allow residents and visitors to wander through my Plot No. 513t to get to Spencer Hole on Mulberry Creek. Just tell them, though, I won't tolerate them stripping any of the berries off my bushes nor leaving any bottles or cans for me to pick up.

And to you, Carl, my best wishes for a happy holiday season and a wonderful New Year. Please keep in touch.

Cordially,

Robert H. Montgomery
Professor

Illustration 5.5 Another Response Letter to Jack Daniel's. Jack Daniel's "Tennessee Squires" become personally involved with the company and act as a brand-loyal unofficial sales force for it. Reprinted courtesy of the writer.

As such, catalog layouts are also a significant showcase for your creative ability since they

- allow full creative play in terms of product positioning, creative approach, layout, creative execution, and copy;

- require a specific theme;

- must meet the challenge of including many items on one page;

- require working a two-page spread as a single layout;

- give all the information required for the sale, as concisely as possible;

- must make every element count in terms of profitability;

- and must combine elements in such a way as to avoid all appearance of clutter or confusion.

Catalogs can be extremely creative in approach, ranging from straight information to the kind of sustained storyline used by Banana Republic; from the upscale traditional look of L.L. Bean to the fast-paced Sharper Image, whose catalog and image represents a consumer and product personality 180 degrees away from the one projected by Jack Daniel's and its catalog. (See Illustration 5.6.)

Within the marketplace, the success of Sharper Image reflects the rapid growth of the entire category, with a contemporary twist: rather than a retail store that branched out into catalog sales, Sharper Image began as a catalog in 1979 before opening its first store two years later. It now has about sixty stores nationwide, with sales topping $200 million. With over 70 percent of its sales coming from men with a median age of 38.9 years and an average household income of $101,200, Sharper Image mailed over 125 million catalogs between 1984 and 1988, with a 1987 average of over thirteen readers per copy.

But whatever the approach, the character of the layout in terms of element size and placement, design motif, typeface, colors used and merchandise presented must reveal the character, quality and pricing of the goods offered. Because catalogs must be specifically targeted, require high creativity, demand consistent and long-term creative strategies, and sorely challenge layout skills, they are an excellent media choice for your creative portfolio.

Magazines

Magazines—and newspapers—come in all types, from consumer fashion-conscious to business engineering-minded, from highly selective to widely

The universe revealed.

Where does the constellation Cassiopeia appear in the midnight sky over New England on December 5? Consult this Starship Earth™ universe globe by Spherical Concepts, and you'll have the answer in seconds. With it, you can reproduce the movements of the earth, sun, and stars at any time, any day of the year, as seen from anywhere on Earth.

Peer through the transparent outer globe and you'll see over 1,100 stars detailed on its inner surface. Stars are shown with their name, Greek letter designation, distance in light years, and brightness.

Arching over the inner earth are 88 ancient and modern constellations. You also see deep sky objects such as open and globular clusters, diffuse and planetary nebula, and galaxies. By rotating the sun ball, you can demonstrate why the sun rises and sets, and the seasons change. Tilt the inner disk to set a horizon line for any location on earth.

Inner globe shows major cities, and latitude and longitude. Outer globe is marked with the astral equivalents used to locate stars, including right ascension lines and sidereal hour angle. Trace star movements with the included wax pencil.

Each beautiful globe is individually hand-blown in the US of clear acrylic. Stainless steel hardware. Measures 16" in diameter; weighs 8 lbs. Mounts on an acrylic desk stand or optional tripod floor stand (32H × 16W"). Includes a 36-page booklet by astronomy expert George Lovi and one-year warranty.

This unusual globe will take you exploring through the fascinating star trails of deep space. Order today.

■ **Starship Earth** #KSP745 $225 (8.50)
■ **Floor Stand** #KSP746 $79 (4.50)

Move cross-country, for the best aerobic workout.

If you've ever spent an afternoon skiing cross-country, you know how invigorated you feel. The smooth, rhythmic movements tone every major muscle group in your body—legs, buttocks, torso, shoulders, and arms. Without the repetitive impact to your body of jogging or aerobics.

Now you can get the fitness and muscle toning benefits of this popular sport at home. Fitness Master™ effectively simulates the actual movements used in cross-country skiing.

Aerobics made easy.

This is the surprise of a Fitness Master workout: *you don't feel like you're working.* You're not straining. Your muscles aren't crying out with pain. Yet within minutes, you can easily elevate your respiration and pulse to the aerobic target rate for your age. Since many muscles are in motion, *less effort is required from each muscle.*

To begin, just step into the cushioned footpads (with or without shoes) and grasp the handgrips. Now, push and pull on the arm poles as you slide your feet back and forth—as if you were gliding across a snow-covered hillside. Repeat this simple 20-minute workout three times a week: 3-minute warm-up, 12 minutes at your target pulse rate, 5-minute cool-down. That's all there is to it.

Built in the US, Fitness Master's chrome-plated steel construction will stand up to many years of rugged use. Non-slip vinyl covers the padded footpads, linked by aircraft cable. Sturdy handlebars adjust to five heights. Folded, measures only 5H × 24½W × 52L"; weighs 36 lbs. Comes with exercise guide and *two-year* warranty.

Feel younger. Look better.

One hour every week working out on Fitness Master can bring profound changes. You'll feel your heart and lungs growing stronger, reducing your risk of cardiovascular disease.

You'll fall asleep easier, sleep better, and wake with more energy. You'll find you can work longer, with less fatigue. And you'll feel a sense of pride in your trim, toned, and healthy body.

Call now to invest in a healthier life. Order Fitness Master for a 30-day trial.

■ **Fitness Master** #KFT350 $449 (25.00)

Illustration 5.6 Direct Mail Catalog Page. Sharper Image uses its stores as hands-on extensions of its dramatically successful direct mail catalog sales. Its name speaks clearly to its target market about the upscale personality and quality of its merchandise. Copyright Sharper Image, 1989. Reprinted courtesy of Sharper Image.

popular. They may be consumer targeted according to popular interest or specific hobby, or business targeted vertically (according to industry) or horizontally (according to level or position within a variety of industries). They command varying amounts of respect and loyalty, and range from superficial and fun loving to serious and intellectually stimulating.

Because magazines are as varied as the population, you can include four-color magazine ads on just about any product, depending on the publication and its target market. But to give the widest possible range to your portfolio, your ads should address a succession of different targets as well as products, including some less obvious choices, such as end-product advertising in business or trade publications. The more highly specialized the publication, the more you must think through the creative strategy in terms of product positioning and creative appeal.

Illustrations 5.7–5.10 for *Field & Stream*, for example, show not only creative strength, but the ability to target a market exactly. Aimed at the media buyer, the ads attempt to gain name awareness and to persuade the reader that *Field & Stream* is an excellent publication to reach the prospective consumer. Note how the illustration (originally run in four-color) clearly identifies the area of interest and compels attention, how the illustration and headline work together to grab the reader, how the body copy follows through with the "sell."

Also notice how the distinctive layout immediately signals the reader that "this is a *Field & Stream* ad," and how everything not relevant to "field" or "stream" has been eliminated, leaving the layout clean and uncluttered. The creative excellence of Peter Warren becomes even clearer here as you realize after seeing the second ad that you are actually looking forward to seeing more.

In writing your own magazine copy, also remember to take advantage of the basic credibility of the medium, its potential for long and informative body copy, and the fact that because publications are so highly targeted, many people read advertising material as avidly as editorial features. Target the publication and reader first, and use this focus to build product image and to address the very specific concerns of your readers through highly informed and specific copy.

Ads appearing in business publications require detailed facts; straightforward, concrete technical information; copy written in the language of the trade and focused on trade or production-specific problems and solutions. Consumer magazines, on the other hand, take a lighter, more conversational tone, and include more of an emotional payoff in addition to the promise of a product benefit. Each approach must be specifically tailored to the target and the editorial environment of the publication.

LOOK AGAIN.

Because of his shape and color, the mule deer blends into the texture of the environment

A closer look will convince you. Field & Stream leads the major men's publications in efficiently reaching the mass male market. With nearly 10 million loyal readers every month, Field & Stream is America's number one sportsman's magazine.

An obvious choice among major men's magazines.

■ We deliver 7.7 million men more efficiently than Time, Newsweek, U.S. News & World Report, Sports Illustrated, Playboy and Penthouse.
■ We deliver men 18-34 more efficiently than Sports Illustrated; men 18-24 more efficiently than Playboy and Penthouse.
■ We deliver $25M + households more efficiently than Time, Newsweek and U.S. News & World Report.

The leader among outdoor magazines.

■ Field & Stream is #1 in: circulation, newsstand sales, total audience, advertising pages and advertising revenue.
■ We deliver more readers than Outdoor Life and Sports Afield combined—and we reach them more efficiently!

■ One ad in Field & Stream reaches nearly 70% of all sportsmen who read the major outdoor magazines—a claim few magazines in *any* field can make.

Field & Stream. The authority in the outdoor field. A leader in the magazine industry with a ninety year tradition of editorial excellence that's stronger than ever. Featuring renowned, award-winning writers like A.J. McClane, George Reiger, Gene Hill, Bob Brister and Ed Zern—authors who continue the rich heritage of great writing established in Field & Stream by the likes of Zane Grey, Ernest Hemingway, Robert Ruark and Erle Stanley Gardner. Reason after reason to look again. Like our readers, you'll be impressed by what you see.

FIELD & STREAM™

America's number one sportsman's magazine.

Field & Stream is a CBS Magazine
Source: 1985 SMRB, ABC, PIB

Illustration 5.7 Magazine Ad. This "Look Again" campaign series, originally run in four-color, (Ills. 5.7–5.10) shows how a powerful illustration, clean layout, and consistent campaign image and focus can involve the reader and perfectly match the medium to the message. Reprinted courtesy of *Field & Stream*.

LOOK AGAIN.

The bird-white quail easily avoids its predators through skillful camouflage.

A closer look will convince you. Field & Stream leads the major men's publications in efficiently reaching the mass male market. With nearly 10 million loyal readers every month, Field & Stream is America's number one sportsman's magazine.

An obvious choice among major men's magazines.

■ We deliver 7.7 million men more efficiently than Time, Newsweek, U.S. News & World Report, Sports Illustrated, Playboy and Penthouse.
■ We deliver men 18-34 more efficiently than Sports Illustrated; men 18-24 more efficiently than Playboy and Penthouse.
■ We deliver $25M + households more efficiently than Time, Newsweek and U.S. News & World Report.

The leader among outdoor magazines.

■ Field & Stream is #1 in: circulation, newsstand sales, total audience, advertising pages and advertising revenue.
■ We deliver more readers than Outdoor Life and Sports Afield combined—and we reach them more efficiently!

■ One ad in Field & Stream reaches nearly 70% of all sportsmen who read the major outdoor magazines—a claim few magazines in *any* field can make.

Field & Stream. The authority in the outdoor field. A leader in the magazine industry with a ninety year tradition of editorial excellence that's stronger than ever. Featuring renowned, award-winning writers like A.J. McClane, George Reiger, Gene Hill, Bob Brister and Ed Zern—authors who continue the rich heritage of great writing established in Field & Stream by the likes of Zane Grey, Ernest Hemingway, Robert Ruark and Erle Stanley Gardner. Reason after reason to look again. Like our readers, you'll be impressed by what you see.

America's number one sportsman's magazine.

Field & Stream is a CBS Magazine.
Source: 1985 SMRB, ABC, PIB.

Illustration 5.8 Magazine Ad

Illustration 5.9 Magazine Ad

LOOK AGAIN.

Few fish can compete with the Brown Trout in utilizing its coloration for efficient camouflage.

A closer look will convince you. Field & Stream leads the major men's publications in efficiently reaching the mass male market. With nearly 10 million loyal readers every month, Field & Stream is America's number one sportsman's magazine.

An obvious choice among major men's magazines.

■ We deliver 7.7 million men more efficiently than Time, Newsweek, U.S. News & World Report, Sports Illustrated, Playboy and Penthouse.
■ We deliver men 18-34 more efficiently than Sports Illustrated; men 18-24 more efficiently than Playboy and Penthouse.
■ We deliver $25M + households more efficiently than Time, Newsweek and U.S. News & World Report.

The leader among outdoor magazines.

■ Field & Stream is #1 in: circulation, newsstand sales, total audience, advertising pages and advertising revenue.
■ We deliver more readers than Outdoor Life and Sports Afield combined—and we reach them more efficiently!

■ One ad in Field & Stream reaches nearly 70% of all sportsmen who read the major outdoor magazines—a claim few magazines in *any* field can make.

Field & Stream. The authority in the outdoor field. A leader in the magazine industry with a ninety year tradition of editorial excellence that's stronger than ever. Featuring renowned, award-winning writers like A.J. McClane, George Reiger, Gene Hill, Bob Brister and Ed Zern—authors who continue the rich heritage of great writing established in Field & Stream by the likes of Zane Grey, Ernest Hemingway, Robert Ruark and Erle Stanley Gardner. Reason after reason to look again. Like our readers, you'll be impressed by what you see.

America's number one sportsman's magazine.

Field & Stream is a CBS Magazine
Source: 1985 SMRB

Illustration 5.10 Magazine Ad

In planning illustrations, think photography—color or black-and-white. Because photographs tend to pull more readership—probably because they capture exactly the way the product looks and works in a realistic setting—they have become more popular than drawings in magazine ads.

In building your own speculative campaign, you may use photographs from existing sources such as government photos available in copyright-free art files in a public library, or even other magazines—provided you bring to the photo your own use and meaning. Don't just "lift" an ad illustration for stain-proof carpeting, for example, and then change the headline and a bit of the copy. Give the photo a whole new interpretation and make a note on the bottom of your copy sheet indicating the original use of the illustration.

Some products or business-to-business ads, however, may work better with four-color graphic designs or abstract illustrations, and the use of photography should always be weighed against the possiblity of other, more effective artistic mediums. Charts and graphs can be a composite of other ads, carefully "X-acto"ed to a clean line and then pasted into position and photocopied afterwards to eliminate the "collage" effect.

In any case, don't mix photos with line drawings in the same ad, and don't allow photos to stray from the product benefit or to draw attention away from, rather than into, your product or service. As with direct mail, always include an item for involving the reader when it's appropriate for the product—a recipe that uses the product, a coupon that gives a price break, a product sample to scratch, sniff, peel, or feel.

Currently the trend is toward breaking the two-dimensional barrier of print with three-dimensional pop-ups, dials to turn, records to play, computer microchip musical inserts—even plastic pouches of artificial snow to evoke the season and the inherent "cool" qualities of the product. Once the province primarily of direct mail, these creative devices have now entered the magazine realm, and even television with the premiere of a "3-D" commercial for Diet Coke during the 1989 Super Bowl.

Although such devices stop the viewer out of curiosity the first time, they are expensive and there is a temptation to use them only as attention gimmicks rather than product benefit enhancers.

Don't give in and use them for their own sake, but when you can find the opportunity to expand the feel or personality of the product into an additional dimension, take it. Being conservative may be a virtue in banking, but your creative book should stretch as far and wide as your imagination. Again, just be sure the product, not the "creative," stays in the limelight.

Newspapers

Newspapers have a more reserved creative character, although there is almost as wide a variety of newspapers as magazines. There are major differences, however, and ads for magazines do not necessarily translate well into newspapers.

While run-of-press (ROP) color is quite good and magazine paper is of a quality at least adequate to support it, most newspapers still rely on black-and-white alone for retail ads. Even though four-color capability is now common among major news publications like *USA Today*, smaller presses still rely on black-and-white, and some larger publications like *The Wall Street Journal* choose it.

Newsprint is also coarser than magazine paper, making a complex halftone (a photograph shot through a screen to break it down into separate dots, later perceived as gradations of black and grey to white on the printed page) impossible, because fine lines and detail would be lost in a blob or be absorbed into a blur on the page.

Consequently, when you design a retail ad, use simple, dominant illustrations of related, grouped merchandise—preferably in line art (black line on a white background). If you use a second or third color, use it sparingly, in one or two single patches that are well placed and chosen according to the nature of the product.

Include plenty of white space to give the eye an oasis in the middle of large amounts of dry editorial matter, and in the copy always include specifics of sale dates, price, directions for getting to the store, hours, featured brand names—as well as any factors which differentiate both the store and its merchandise from the competition. Feature the store name prominently, and give the reader a reason to either "buy now" or patronize that particular shop.

Illustration 5.11 is an example of the effective use of line drawing, white space, and the power of visual metaphor in a newspaper ad to convey product benefit. In this case, the advertiser—an advertising agency—addresses a benefit meaningful to many potential clients fearful of being lost in insignificance, shortchanged in a conflict of interests, or dwarfed by the bureaucratic tangles implied by current agency megamergers. The ad's simplicity, clarity, and directness not only hit the "suffering point" exactly, but serve as an example of the agency's creative excellence as well.

Transit car cards

Don't dismiss transit car cards from your media list. They have excellent advertising capabilities: the audience is captive for about twenty minutes or

Illustration 5.11 Black and White Newspaper Ad. The simplicity of this design, its visual metaphor and line drawing execution is perfectly suited to the newspaper medium and to the form and content of the message. Reprinted courtesy of Miller Meyers Bruce Dalla Costa.

longer each ride, and they are usually embarrassed to look anywhere else but at car cards or their own newspapers. As a result, you can include a lot of body copy, graphically explain or illustrate concepts or products, and count on repeated exposures.

Readers are also psychologically attuned to ads that stress solutions to major suffering points they may be feeling at the time. Rush hour commuters, for example, are usually tired, hungry, frustrated, and especially susceptible to offers of change. What better place to address someone about new employment or educational opportunities than when they are thinking about how angry or frustrated they are with their jobs or bosses? Include a packet of tear-away coupons or application/information blanks so that they, like drivers observing outdoor posters, can respond as soon as possible to your offer.

Transit car cards are also an excellent medium to advertise points of sale along the route: restaurants, stores, entertainment centers, etc.—all these are right outside the window and obviously convenient for travelers already on the car or bus. Include as much information as you like, but in a point size easy to read from three or four feet.

Remember, however, that outside transit has completely different characteristics and should follow the format of outdoor posters in terms of readily noticed and understood illustrations and easy-to-read copy.

Broadcast Media
Radio

Radio, as a completely different medium, represents another kind of creative challenge. Not only are we usually busy with something else while we're listening, but we also never see the product in use, the way we can in print or on television. Effective radio commercials must break through the clutter of other commercials and through listener consciousness as well, by becoming so sensually specific and appealing that the listener will pay attention and let his or her imagination create its own picture. Radio's greatest asset is your imagination.

Some radio ads settle for using "bells and whistles" to gain attention but then fade into a kind of audio wallpaper. Great radio commercials use highly selective sounds associated with the product and its benefit to suggestively seduce the imagination—sounds of ice dropped into a glass, for example, or background sounds of laughter and pool splashing—to maximize the audio potential of the medium and to overcome its visual limitations.

Illustration 5.12 shows a typical radio script format as well as a now-classic ad for the benefits of radio. Written by Stan Freberg, the radio ad for radio itself shows how the combination of an exceptionally creative mind and an advertising medium can successfully seduce the imagination and turn an apparent shortcoming of the medium into a strength.

If you include a radio ad in your portfolio, pay very close attention to more than just background or "prop" sounds. Read the commercial aloud to detect impossible sound combinations—as with the *s*'s in the last sentence of the previous paragraph—as well as to over-long audio sentences—like this one. Stay within standard time limits, and when writing, use the appropriate format.

Television

Television is a highly specialized medium, one often not represented at all in creative books, unless the person is experienced in television production, or the ad is a significant part of a larger campaign. As mentioned earlier, unless you know exactly what you're doing, leave it out.

Media Positioning

Because each medium has its own personality, then, it's important to remember that just as people judge others by their companions and the neighborhoods they live in, people will also judge your product or service by the media company it keeps. This means extending the concept of product positioning, which matches product and user personalities, to include media positioning as well.

Effective advertising matches product benefit, user personality, and media personality so that the message reaches the target as clearly and directly as possible. When the match isn't exact, the message can't achieve full potential impact. If, for example, you have an expensive food product like truffles to sell, you risk cheapening it by giving it a "full showing" (placing it in every car) in a transit ad. Placing a four-color ad in *Bon Appetit* or *Gourmet* magazine, however, puts your product right among the people who will best appreciate its advantages. Don't put your product into an environment where it misses its prospective purchasers or may look less appealing to them.

Think long and hard about matching your product or service's characteristics to your target market, your target market to the media to which it is exposed, and your message and creative execution to the appropriate media.

Client:	Radio Advertising Bureau
Copy:	Stan Freberg

MAN: Radio? Why should I advertise on radio? There's nothing to look at. No pictures.

FREBERG: Listen, you can do things on radio you couldn't possibly do on TV.

MAN: That'll be the day.

FREBERG: All right, watch this. (clears voice) OK, people, and now when I give you the cue, I want the 700-foot mountain of whipped cream to roll into Lake Michigan which has been drained and filled with hot chocolate. Then the Royal Canadian Air Force will fly overhead, towing a 10-ton maraschino cherry which will be dropped into the whipped cream to the cheering of 25,000 extras. All-l-l right, cue the mountain!

SFX: *(massive rumbling followed by huge splash)*

FREBERG: Cue the Air Force!

SFX: *(drone of planes)*

FREBERG: Cue the maraschino cherry!

SFX: *(long whistle and dull splash)*

FREBERG: OK, 25,000 cheering extras!

SFX: *(enormous crowd roar)*

FREBERG: Now, do you want to try that on television?

MAN: We-e-ell.

FREBERG: You see, radio's a very special medium because it stretches the imagination.

MAN: Doesn't television stretch the imagination?

FREBERG: Up to 21 inches, ye-e-es.

Illustration 5.12   Radio Commercial. This classic radio commercial by Stan Freberg illustrates both format and how good writing can make us "see" and hear the creative benefits of radio as an advertising medium. Copyright 1964, 1986, Radio Advertising Bureau. Reprinted courtesy of RAB.

6

Rules

This chapter addresses those readers who want to know why there are "rules" in advertising, especially because they have heard so often—something like this is even mentioned in the opening note of this book—that there *aren't* any rules for good creative work. Well, the truth is that there *are* rules, and that when the rules are violated, the price is paid in not communicating your advertising message. In fact, the basic "rules" can be reduced to two fundamental and commonsense concepts:

- use what communicates effectively;

- avoid what doesn't.

But how do you determine what communicates effectively and what doesn't? So far, you have read advice ("rules," if you will) based on the practical experience of people who judge creative portfolios and the effectiveness of their contents. Much of this advice is based both on research and intuition, the result of professional research studies and of unconsciously absorbing creative advertising patterns that have worked for advertisers themselves or for their competitors.

But because research yields data for answers and not the answers themselves, and because people often draw different conclusions from the same data, it may be helpful to turn to some basic psychological principles of perception and communication to understand how these basic rules operate, and therefore how they can eventually be twisted, stretched, pushed and pulled into advertisements and campaigns which perfectly marry your creative genius to the product message. The "rules" are really only practical guidelines based on principles of communication and perceptual process.

These principles themselves show us how to eventually "break the rules" by revealing the spirit behind the letter of the "law." When you understand the universal principle of keeping the integrity of the whole within the unique creative idea, you can stop worrying about rigid guidelines. Then when you "break the rules," you do so by conforming to a higher law, not just because you don't know what you're doing. But while working on transcending the rules, remember that they are important and useful guidelines for people who haven't yet fully grasped the nuances of the principle.

Advertising, as an attempt to communicate a specific product message to a specifically targeted consumer, always involves a message, a sender, a medium, and a receiver. In previous chapters, concepts of product positioning (sender/receiver compatibility) and media characteristics were discussed. But just as important as those concepts is the process of understanding *how* messages are perceived, for the ad must be just as compatible with the perceptual process of the message receiver as the product benefit itself is with his/her felt needs. The same principles govern them all. Here are some of the most important.

Ads as Gestalts

The word *gestalt*, taken directly from the German and defined by Webster as "a physical, psychological, or symbolic configuration or pattern so unified as a whole that its properties cannot be derived from its parts," has significant meaning for advertising, because it provides the principle underlying the means by which the elements of an ad—the illustration, headline, body copy, logo, layout, and eye path—work together to create a total effect or impression of the product or service being advertised.

The key to its significance lies in its recognition of the role that relationship plays in creating meaning—that is, in how the form and placement of each element affects each of the others in achieving a single, stable message impact.

The early Gestalt psychologists focused on learning; and in various perceptual experiments with animals and human beings, they found that "insight," the point at which a problem was solved, involved a sudden grasp, not of the meaning of separate things in themselves, but of relationships among things.

They realized that the relationship between parts as they came together created an energy, and a new and different meaning from anything which existed in the separate parts themselves. And they recognized that the moment when the relationship was perceived was the moment of making sense—and therefore of memorability.

They also observed that the process of forming insights through perception of relationships was both universal and automatic. Though subject to the influence of immediate needs and cultural and social differences, the formation of insights, they saw, operates the same way in all people—simply as a result of evolution and the need to survive in a world where our senses are constantly being bombarded by complex stimuli.

In short, Gestalt psychologists have shown that universal perceptual principles organize what we see into meaningful messages. If there are not enough elements or clues to form a coherent message, a state of perceptual tension is created that demands resolution; when the whole comes together, tension is relaxed and a stable memory trace is formed.

In other words, if we are given enough information, and the information all tends in the same direction, we will form a conclusion and continue to remember it. Without enough information, the process remains open to change by other influence and is therefore easily forgotten or changed.

This is why ads where all the elements work together toward a common purpose are remembered, while ads where elements are vague, unrelated, or leading off into different directions are easily forgotten, or only those elements which seem to make sense are remembered. In a truly effective ad, when one element is changed, the whole meaning of the ad changes; and when even one element works against the message, it loses memorability.

Tension and Closure

The final coming together of the elements into a stable whole—the process of psychological "closure"—not only alleviates tension in its own context, but also acts as a catharsis to other accumulated tensions as well. This may be why many people tend to identify the purchase of things with emotional satisfactions sought in other parts of their lives, and why they really do feel better when they buy something.

When an ad communicates its message clearly and effectively—when its message is remembered and its benefit is powerful enough to motivate purchase of the product, it generates "insight": the product is seen as a solution to the particular consumer problem.

This in turn generates further tension as the consumer is moved to buy the product to resolve the problem. And as the solution of one problem tends to relieve other accumulated, but perhaps vague and undefined, tensions, the purchase provides further catharsis for these as well.

Each ad exists as a perceptual whole whose meaning depends on appropriate product positioning and the creative choices made in putting together the layout. Creative strategy therefore implies not only effective targeting, but also tight artistic control in being able to generate and relax tension through the choice and placement of elements. Once the elements are on the page, they take on a life of their own, as the forces at work within the ad take over to form their own meaning, according to their own "inner necessity" and the needs of the reader.

If they are well planned and come together as a gestalt meaningfully targeted to the needs of a specific audience, the effect will be one of power and "internal integrity." Let them fight one another for dominance or "sense," and the ad will achieve little or no impact at all.

Creatively and ethically "cheap" psychological closure

The ability of advertising to generate psychological tension and to generate product purchase as a solution accounts for its power—and as a result, for its attendant creative ethical responsibility. Because much of the art of advertising involves identifying a consumer problem and showing how the product will solve it, the temptation is to target the prime motivating factors in human behavior, like the sex drive and hunger, and then to artificially attach products as an apparent solution to them. This is what the "sex sell" attempts to do, and also why it doesn't work.

"Image" advertising is also relevant in that it suggests an impression of a life-style and satisfactions in relation to products that may in fact have quite different consequences, such as liquor and cigarettes. Although products can easily attach an artificially glamorous image to themselves, if their purchase cannot solve the problems on which the ad focuses or provide the satisfactions implied by the image, the consumer is left only wanting more of a vague "something" rather than your product, and feeling less adequate about himself or herself.

It's advertising at its cheapest—and not the way to advertise any product with a real benefit, or to advertise your own talent by including such ads in your book.

Making Sense of It All

An ad finally makes sense to us through the workings of the Gestalt "Law of Prägnanz," the most important and fundamental Gestalt law of perception. Simply stated, it explains that all perceptual stimuli will be reduced to their simplest and "best" forms. This means that in order to make sense of what we see, our minds reduce complex visual data into the most basic patterns and shapes. When these shapes are not complete or perfect in themselves, we tend to complete them (closure) as if the same line were followed to its logical conclusion (good continuation).

A near or incomplete circle, for example, is seen by us as a "circle" rather than as a line of varying arc. The process works automatically. For advertisers, this means that by suggesting a strong enough pattern (internal logic or line of good continuation), they can show a part of a story and rely on the reader to complete it. By showing a 30-second television commercial, for example, and later repeating a part of it in fifteen seconds, the viewer will mentally fill in the rest, in the same way that we can make people laugh by saying only the punchline of a joke they know.

It's also why "lift-outs" of frames from television commericals work well as point-of-purchase advertising, and why in print advertising, we can focus on a part of something—a story or a person or a product—and if it is representative enough to imply the rest, the reader's imagination will fill in what's missing.

The trick, of course, is to say or include just enough to make the reader or viewer complete the story in exactly the way you want him to. Leave out too much and there's confusion—confusion which is perhaps most easily solved by turning the page. Establish no clear line of perception to follow and the reader may finish the message in a way you might regret, as in a headline question ("Want to make more money?") which invites a "wisecrack" response ("Who me? Naaaaah.").

Closely allied to the problem of ambiguity is the use of opposites to provoke maximum tension, which the product then resolves. For example, an outdoor poster featuring an illustration of a man lying on the beach at rest, with the headline "men at work" to the side, certainly provokes interest. But because it doesn't make sense, we continue to look for the element which will make it all come together. This is both an advertising asset and a drawback, because it stretches closure to its very limits.

In the case of an outdoor poster, by the time we have caught the conflict, we've probably already passed the poster, and therefore never see the identifying mark of the product or service which would bring the two together. In the case of a magazine or newspaper ad, the opposites and the product-as-synthesis have to be so creatively tight as to be a perfect triad. If the apparent opposites aren't resolved by the product, we just get annoyed at the gimmickry.

The key to effective advertising lies in getting exactly the right involvement between the reader and product through tension and closure. With too few clues, the process is left open to other forces, or to a disintegration of interest. With too much stated, not enough tension is generated for the reader to become involved in the product message.

Notice how the *Field & Stream* ad campaign shown earlier (see Illustrations 5.7–5.10) is able to grab attention, generate reader involvement, integrate visual and verbal elements, and communicate with the desired prospect.

Layout and gestalt formation

In terms of layout, the process of gestalt formation implies that if we allow too much space between elements that should be perceived as parts in a whole, these elements will tend to separate from one another, and the result is a confusion of numbers. Things seem to "drift" on the page or to "fall" off it.

Elements can be made to seem alike, however, through proximity, repetition of shape, or color; and an eye path can be consciously established to lead from one element into the next, until all the elements are pulled together into a single whole. Proximity and likeness = association; space and dissimilarity = dissociation.

When the parts fight each other because of differences between "the sell" and the various elements of tone, composition, purpose, personality, product differentiation, medium, typeface, headline content, body copy support, etc., the ad loses impact because it disintegrates into separate sections with apparently different purposes. The result is that not only does the ad lack the power to break through the clutter of the competition, but it also in effect creates its own "clutter"—it divides itself and conquers its own purpose before the competition even gets started.

Reduction and expansion

Reduction and expansion means that only essential words and images should be used in an ad. Details external to the product message become mere decorations which distract from the message. If, for example, the ad is meant to show the benefit of a particular eye cream in smoothing wrinkles, is it necessary to show the woman's earrings? The more artful the omission of unimportant detail, the more involving the ad is to the imagination because it allows it to focus on the significant without any distraction.

Notice how the advertising agency ad (Illustration 5.11) uses the combination of visual and verbal metaphor to focus on the significant and how the *Field & Stream* ads (Illustrations 5.7–5.10) utilize the perceptual process of discrimination between figure and ground to intrigue the reader into the body copy.

Words and images must also be made to fit together to suggest a larger story to which the person can relate through experience or even by identifying with the protagonist. In addition, the reader also must be persuaded that the product promise is true. This means expansion as well as reduction, because the body copy must include details representative enough to conjure a whole situation meaningful to the reader, yet specific and forceful enough to motivate the purchase.

In effective body copy, specific statistics can be used to achieve this by focusing on the problem, varying the examples of the same theme in word and image, eliminating the insignificant and substantiating the claim with relevant and representative information.

7

The Role of Layout Elements

Breaking through the Clutter—Achieving Readability and Memorability

Attracting Notice

Before any ad can be perceptually "read," it must first be noticed. Although each day we are barraged by approximately 1,500 ads, only a very small percentage enter our consciousness. Like all other stimuli which impinge on our senses, advertisements are screened by an automatic selective perception process. Only those ads which speak directly to our immediate felt needs or to our perceived long-term self-interest—and which do so in the first few seconds of exposure—make it through our mental screening process.

Because of this, major print advertising research services focus first on the noticeability of the ad to measure its effectiveness. Starch, for example, rates print ads on "Noted," "(Advertiser) Associated," and "Read Most" (of the copy). Gallup and Robinson measures "Proved Name Registration" and "Favorable Buying Attitude."

Both researchers in print ad effectiveness look first for the ad's ability to stop the reader, because an ad cannot effectively sell unless it is first noticed; and then for reader association of the ad with its sponsor, because if the reader doesn't link the two, the client loses a potential customer.

Although ultimately neither company can measure whether the ad did its final job of selling its product, service, or idea with anything close to certainty (direct response advertising comes closest to this ideal), nevertheless both recognize the fact that an ad cannot sell unless it first reaches out and grabs the reader's interest. It is this concentration on reader awareness that makes advertising's use of visual language so important: it is the visual illustration that is first and most easily read, and which tells us whether or not the ad is directed at our own individual interest.

Visually Speaking

The visual content of the illustration attracts us not only because it consists of recognizable items and colors, but also because of its visual grammar and syntax, which act just as the Gestalt Law of Prägnanz does in reducing things to their most basic, pleasing, and meaningful shapes. That is, we not only see things, but also their subjects, objects, and relationships. Their meaning is completed by us along the line of our experience (or our fantasies) precisely as it is suggested by the internal line of logic within the illustration.

It works in the same manner as the first few notes of a melody, by leading us to anticipate the whole and to become emotionally caught up in it.

Each of the details in an advertisement is like a musical note; the melody—the relationship pulling the notes together—is the meaningful gestalt. If the melody is familiar, we keep the whole of it in our minds while we hear the parts. If it is unfamiliar, the line begun by the first few notes already suggests to us how it might be developed. In this way, each part of an effective ad suggests and anticipates every other, building and reinforcing rather than just repeating over and over. (This inherent unity and development is, of course, part of the reason for the creative impact of the Jack Daniel's direct mail campaign—its recipients truly look forward with delight to how the product personality will emerge in the next creative piece.)

The resulting visual language of each ad therefore expresses meanings contained both within the illustration and, as it involves us by its meaningfulness in our own concerns, within the larger context of our individual and social lives. An ad's visual language performs the same function in the commercial marketplace that symbolism performs in literature and poetry.

As a result, it may, in fact, be possible to build a satisfactory personality profile of a person simply by knowing the images associated with the products and services the person uses—just as effective product positioning matches product and consumer personality. The science of archaeology and product positioning are based on the same premise: we come to know people by the things they use.

Good ads thus take full advantage of existing universal and cultural symbols to create images for their products which in turn imply meaningful experience. As with statements in verbal language, ad illustrations and layouts suggest ideas and associations. They evoke feelings about ourselves, others and our environment. They define us to ourselves and to others.

Print as illustration

The visual language of advertisements is also more concise and more quickly and easily grasped than their verbal language, which consists of a series of complex lines in the forms of letters and words. Headlines and body copy, as symbols which must be read and interpreted, are more abstract and therefore more difficult to process than pictures, which are sensed as reflections of our own visual reality. Illustrations speak directly to the emotions, and their meaning is understood through a perceptually streamlined process.

Despite the importance of visuals, advertisers often make the mistake of disregarding their importance as a primary means of gaining message impact. Witness, for example, the growing trend toward the use of headlines as illustrations.

When words are substituted for images, the result is usually not effective communication, but interesting graphic design—aesthetically appealing, perhaps, but without the immediate impact of a visual message. This is especially true when lines are joined at top and bottom and done in all capitals. Unless the headline is a simple word or two, set in lower case, and has strong news value or irresistible curiosity appeal, it cannot achieve the full power and immediacy of a visual.

Note how the advertising creative workshop of Illustration 7.1 utilizes this weakness of print-as-illustration to make its point through creative professional humor. (In spoofing itself, of course, it must ironically hope that it does not fall victim to its own technique!)

Dominance

Good visuals don't just happen with artwork or photography, however. They must be consciously structured to make perception easy. For example, Gestalt psychologists tell us that for a "figure" to stand out against its "ground," there must be enough contrast between them: figures are created by a center of interest and a pulling force of uniformity of shape, size, proximity and similarity; and they are segregated from their backgrounds by contrast in these.

For ease of perception, then, the product should appear as a dominant "figure" (product, person, combination) that stands out easily from the simpler surface against which it is seen. When advertisers don't create a single dominant illustration or regular pattern, or if they don't use a single, dominant area of color in two- or three-color ads, the result can be confusion as to what to look at first, along with a sense of annoyance at the clutter distracting attention from the message—a single message which should be both attractive and reinforced visually and verbally.

Reverse type

Visually, "reverse type"—white lettering on a black background—which has become extremely popular in current ad layouts, can also work effectively only when it is confined to a very few words and is large enough to read comfortably.

Although the predominance of black may achieve visual impact from a design standpoint, it lacks the ability to communicate simply, because it lacks ease of readability. The contrast is there, but the effect is reversed, with the black so overwhelming that the print is extremely difficult to read. (Note Illustration 7.1 again from this point of view.) From at least school age on, we are used to reading black letters on a light ground.

In a four-color ad, the problem of reverse type is compounded even more. As the press spins off thousands of imprints each minute, the likelihood of the copy going slightly out of register is quite high. The result? Not crisply defined white letters, but muddy and obscure configurations with halos of magenta, cyan, or yellow. Although it is true that color separation and print production methods continue to improve and may eventually eliminate the problem entirely, reverse type is still too difficult to read in body copy and should be avoided.

Similarly, print that runs over the illustration doesn't allow the print as "figure" to stand out from the "ground." If the layout as a whole is filled with visual or verbal clutter, or if it appears too difficult or too confusing to read, it just won't be read. And if it won't be read, why put it in?

Visuals as message simplifiers

Thus, the visual language of illustration and layout not only opens the communication process with the reader by signaling the target market that the ad is directed at its needs, but it also works to visually reduce complex product

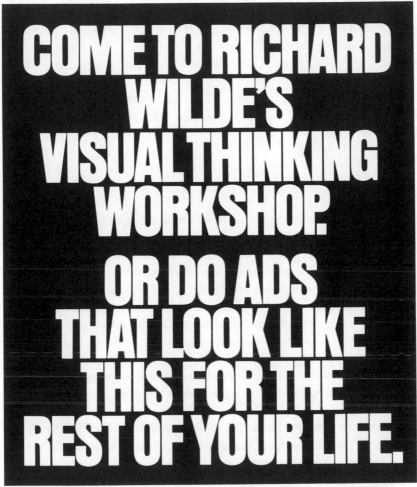

COME TO RICHARD WILDE'S VISUAL THINKING WORKSHOP.

OR DO ADS THAT LOOK LIKE THIS FOR THE REST OF YOUR LIFE.

Richard Wilde is the Chairman of Graphic Design and Advertising at the School of Visual Arts, and the author of the popular book—Problems/Solutions. He teaches people to abandon existing formulas for approaching problems and think much more visually.

His day-long workshop consisting of a series of assignments will help you to think more visually and expand your mind. All without the help of any hallucinogenic drugs.

To sign up for Mr. Wilde's workshop, call the Ad Club at (617) 262-1100. RICHARD

WILDE'S VISUAL THINKING WORKSHOP. THE WESTIN HOTEL, 10 HUNTINGTON AVE., BOSTON, MA. WEDNESDAY, JANUARY 11, 1989. 8:30 AM—registration/continental breakfast. 9 AM–4:30 PM—workshop.
Cost $195 for Ad Club

members, $250 for all non-members. Cancellations accepted until 5 pm Friday, Jan. 6. Price includes breakfast, coffee break, and lunch. Space limited to 50 people.

The AdClub
THE ADVERTISING CLUB OF GREATER BOSTON

Illustration 7.1 Print as Illustration. This ad, directed at advertising creatives, attacks the lack of creativity in using print as illustration and makes its point through a humorous reversal in both type and creative concept. Reprinted courtesy of Leonard Monahan Lubars & Partners.

benefit statements to visual metaphors which simplify the message and thereby achieve emphasis.

The most effective visualizations depict a positive emotional environment and suggest a story in which the reader relates to the protagonist. These ads so closely associate the company name and reputation, the product and its benefit, and the reader's need and self-interest, that they merge into a single image. When this happens, the image has not only achieved product "name registration," but it has also emotionally involved the reader in the message and paved the way for product satisfaction through enhancement of the reader's self-image.

Positives and negatives

Closely related to this is the tendency of people to block out negative messages both consciously and unconsciously. When we understand this, it is then no surprise to learn that "scare" ads—such as those originally done by the American Cancer Society using fear as a motivation to quit smoking— just don't work as well as ads which use a positive approach by offering simple and palatable solutions to the problem—such as the ads done by a popular cereal that related studies on fiber and cancer prevention to its own product.

By emphasizing a wife's concern for her husband's health (this is how to be a good wife), the fact that she could do something positive about it (you can play an active and positive role in his world), and the fact that the cereal was easy to serve and tasted good (all you have to do is buy the product and add milk to make a healthful contribution to your future together), the ad focused on the positive control of disease and reinforced a positive self-image as well—despite its use of the much-feared word, *cancer*.

Ads as ads

In understanding the positive and negative psychological impact of advertising's visual and verbal language, then, it is especially important to recognize advertising's role in a larger communication context, for product users are not only product benefit purchasers, they are also self-identification seekers and self-identification promoters as well. They buy products and services which are not only useful to them but which, in being used, also confirm their own self-images and in turn send out meaningful messages about themselves to others. The principle applies equally to everyone in any materialistic society, from alligator emblem-wearers to "punk rockers."

In this process, effective advertisements can and do create specific and definite symbols. Through repetition these symbols become generally recognized by the public and can be used to send out secondary messages through product use. If a certain brand of blue jeans can effectively position itself as "young, sexy and on-the-move," for example, those same jeans, in being worn, will send out the signal that the wearer is also "young, sexy, and on-the-move." The same, of course, is true of status automobiles, celebrity-endorsed cosmetics, and orange juice.

When a product or service has been successfully "positioned"—i.e., perfectly matched in consumer personality and product benefit—consumers associate the product with an image of themselves which they either possess or wish to project, or both, and then use the positioning to make statements about themselves in terms of personality or social status. In short, successful ads create images that consumers can then use to advertise themselves. Without effective product positioning to establish a specific, positive product image, this would be impossible.

Verbally Speaking

Although it is the illustration that initially grabs consumers' attention, emotionally involving them and suggesting the product benefit, the role of copy—verbally building on and reinforcing the message, linking the visual to the verbal, naming the brand, and defining and supporting the product benefit—is equally important.

To be effective, the headline must clarify the reader's interpretation of the illustration and complement its visual shorthand with a concise verbal promise of a consumer benefit. In this respect, the headline of advertising copy is like poetry in its economy of expression and reliance on imagery. It is an imagistic bridge between the visual illustration and the verbal body copy.

If the headline contradicts the visual message of the illustration, the resulting opposition essentially forces the reader to choose between them, or to abandon the ad altogether as simply too much bother to understand. Cigarette advertising, for example, capitalizes on this by using a healthful and positive visual illustration to dominate the verbal warning. Dominant illustration, preference for the positive, and ease of processing visual over verbal language combine to render the negative message insignificant.

Teaser headlines

Sometimes the visual or headline may take a "teaser" approach in the hope that although readers cannot identify themselves or their needs in it, the creative approach is so intriguing that sheer curiosity itself will pull them into the body copy for the answer. As a creative technique, a curiosity-arousing headline can work well if the curiosity factor is closely tied to the product benefit and the illustration, or if it suggests that something new is occurring that is meaningful to the reader. But if it *only* arouses curiosity, it is a highly risky closure technique, because most of the body copy is rarely read.

Avoid it as a creative approach because so much is against its getting the message across:

- it fails to target the market through self-interest;
- it doesn't involve the reader in the benefit immediately;
- it risks communication shut-off if gratification is too delayed;
- it misdirects interest toward the creative instead of the product;
- and it loses the opportunity of gaining product name recognition in the casual page-turner.

Headlines as pure poetry

When, however, the headline succeeds in extending the illustration into words by verbally repeating and reinforcing the product benefit seen in the illustration, the headline smoothes the message and leads the reader into the body copy. In this respect, both illustration and headline are *synecdochic*, to borrow a term from poetry. That is, they use visual and verbal imagery focusing on the part of the "product story" that implies the rest—in the same way that "hands" can be used to imply "workers" in phrases like "all hands on deck," or a two-thirds line drawing of a circle will imply the rest of it.

The more specifically focused, concrete, and suggestive the illustration and headline are, the more effectively they will communicate. The same is also true of body copy. If the wording is too vague to conjure up a mental image, it will not encourage imaginative involvement on the part of the reader.

Like the headline serving as the bridge between the visual illustration and the verbal body copy, the copy itself must also be imagistic and synecdochic—that is, it must use language related to the central metaphor of the visual, and give facts and figures which imply the rest of the product story. Illustration, headline and body copy must work visually and verbally to reinforce a product image matched to the image of the target market.

Again, notice how the Miller Myers Bruce Dalla Costa ad (Illustration 5.11) relates visual to verbal in illustration and headline through the use of metaphor, and how the specific copy of Freberg's radio ad (Illustration 5.12) works on the imagination to create a vivid mental image which perfectly illustrates the precise benefit offered by the medium that it is advertising.

Colorfully speaking

All colors have connotative codes derived from either nature or the culture in which they occur. The Jolly Green Giant is green for a reason—we expect vegetables to be packaged in green because in nature, green says "fresh, natural." Red is as exciting to the eye as fire is to experience. A beige can says "frosty root beer"; a deep red one says "full-bodied and rich." Black says "upscale elegance."

So if you decide to package chocolate milk in a white carton with green and orange lettering, you shouldn't be surprised if the people who pour out what they thought would be orange juice the next morning will get angry enough not to buy the product again. They will simply pass over your product and reach for the more obvious chocolate drink—the one in the brown carton or with chocolate lettering.

Always stop to research and think about color before you use it. Make sure that it is fully synthesized with the rest of the product message in terms of product identity and consumer psychology. Use full color to gain higher readership through realism in magazine ads; use a spot of well-chosen and well-placed color in black-and-white ads for reader attention and product recognition. But always use it consciously and deliberately.

Implied Ifs and Don'ts

You should familiarize yourself with advertising and marketing research, reported in such sources as the *Journal of Advertising Research* and the *Journal of Marketing Research*, and read trade journals, such as *Advertising Age* and *AD-*

WEEK, in order to understand developing marketing, advertising, and consumer trends, especially in terms of business outlooks and socioeconomic, life-style, and buying patterns. These will help you avoid misdirecting your ads by using obsolete demographic and psychographic assumptions and formulaic approaches to specific consumer problems.

However, as we have seen, there are some basic perceptual and communication rules which enable certain appeals and layouts to work, regardless of trends and shifting patterns.

As with any effective communication,

- the print ad message should be aimed at a specific purpose,

- the message should be written in easily understood visual and verbal language,

- omission or suggestibility should be used judiciously to trigger reader involvement,

- visual and verbal imagery should be designed to be mutually complementary and involving,

- visual interference should be eliminated from the design of the ad.

With this in mind, here is a list of some of the major common creative approaches that **don't** work and therefore should be **avoided**:

- brag and boast appeals, like "We're Number 1!" which don't relate to consumer self-interest;

- gimmicks such as trick headlines, crazy pictures, colored words, excessive use of tint blocks, etc., which distract from the product or interfere with the benefit message;

- copy or visuals that focus on more than one benefit. The result of trying to put everything in the ad is confusion, lack of impact, and weak product benefit identification. Each ad should focus on only one main benefit, the one most meaningful to your target market;

- including too many elements of any sort—too many visuals, too many typefaces—which create a confusing message or layout;

- failure to mention the product name or the benefit in the headline. Remember that it may be all that is read;

- illustrations and headlines that fail to target a specific market. They won't listen if they don't know you're talking to them;

- negative appeals focusing on what the product hasn't fixed yet or on what happens if you don't use it. The negative will invariably associate itself with your product. If you use a "before," use an "after";

- sex for attention or its own sake, drawing attention away from product benefit;

- questions that leave answers open and thus invite answers that are wise-cracks or satiric sallies;

- headlines split or in all capitals; reverse type, especially in body copy; italics and decorative type in general; and headlines or body copy sur-printed over the illustration—all of which make the ad so difficult to read that it may not be read at all.

The most successful ads visually and verbally target the consumer personality exactly, act as extensions and refinements of the product message, and suggest a storyline which the targeted consumer completes in his or her own imagination. This pattern of visual suggestion and psychological closure makes the illustration and complementary headline and body copy work simultaneously on both the emotional and the rational level.

On the emotional level, the ad gets reader attention through self-identification or interest value, and reader involvement through closure as he or she completes the ad "story."

On the rational level, the illustration simplifies the product message and appeals to the rational self-interest of the reader through the specifically defined product benefit. The headline and body copy verbally reinforce this, and all the ad elements come together around the product benefit, which is seen as a solution to the problem.

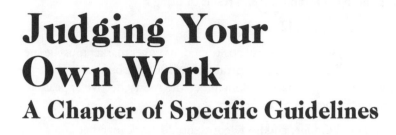

Judging Your
Own Work
A Chapter of Specific Guidelines

The following lists of guidelines are meant as reminders of concepts of which you should already be aware, but which sometimes are overlooked in the excitement of a creative idea. None of the guidelines represents an inviolable rule, but you must know exactly why you are ignoring it and realize that readership of your ad may be jeopardized if the lure of "creativity" is too strong.

Approaching the Ad as a Creative Whole

- Make it clear at a glance what the product is and what its benefit is. It may be all the time you may have to communicate it.

- Show what the product looks like, so that it can be readily recognized in the store.

- Make sure the creative is subordinate to the product identity and the benefit message. The benefit should be unique or better than the competition in some way significant to the consumer.

- Focus on the single, broadest, most meaningful appeal to your target market. Be sure, too, that it isn't also applicable to the competition's product. Focus on your solution to the most common, significant consumer problem and on the end result of using it.

- Make sure the ad SELLS.

- The product should be clearly positioned: its target market must be specific and well chosen, and the product benefit must be clear and meaningful to the target market. Remember the most effective appeals are savings in money, time, and effort.

- Illustration, headline, and body copy should work together as a single unit, stressing a single benefit. Repeat the benefit through the illustration, in the headline, and in three different ways in your body copy. Give enough support to the benefit to make it believable.

- The approach should be original, interesting, and capable of breaking through ad clutter. Humor works well if it has a light touch and works on a broad and basic human level. Think twice about using it if you're a novice, however. It's the hardest thing to do well—it just misses too often. Never take an approach that is insulting or degrading, and be sure the product stays in the spotlight.

- Use situations that suggest a story and with which the reader can identify quickly and easily. Use the unusual and the unexpected to gain interest.

- Don't forget that you're addressing the buyer of the product, not necessarily the ultimate user of the product.

- Appeal to the senses.

- Key the approach, illustration, and copy to the editorial environment of the publication.

- Avoid stereotypes and looking or sounding like other ads.

- Make sure of the appropriateness of the
  —visual to product benefit,
  —typeface to product and target market,
  —basic layout design to product and benefit,
  —copy approach and tone to product and target market.

- The campaign theme should be consistent throughout, but with interesting variations.

- Use coupons and recipes to involve the reader in the product benefit and add a buying incentive.

- Use color whenever possible to gain attention and brand recognition, and remember that all colors have connotative meanings.

- Don't be lured into a "brag and boast" approach.

- Reward the reader with useful information, light humanistic humor, or inner satisfaction.

- Make it easy to read and to understand.

Visual Guidelines

Layout

- In two-page spreads, remember that the fold will take space, thereby distorting illustrations, spaces, and letters. Design the fold into the layout.

- Use good design sense in space and balance. Keep pale elements above, and place dark or heavy elements, such as copy blocks, at the bottom.

- Don't leave a layout in exact, geometric balance: it stops dead. Divide the layout into zones of three, horizontally and vertically, not into mirrored halves, and assign points of interest where they will create some tension for interest, but not so much that the result is confusion or division.

- Ads should be kept as open and light as possible, especially technical ads. The more complex the product, the simpler the layout should be and the longer the body copy should be.

- Remember that white space is the least used, most effective way of creating emphasis and readability. Make sure, however, that you don't separate elements that belong together. If the white border you use in mounting your ads is an important part of the balance of the layout, then reduce the layout and include the margin of space within it.

- Keep it simple and strong. Never clutter the layout with more visuals than necessary. Every additional visual stimulus represents a loss in overall impact.

- Use people in consumer ads, but only in some meaningful connection to the product—never as decoration. In industrial, trade, and professional ads, use charts, schematics, graphs, tables, cross-sections, etc., because your target is accustomed to reading them, and they can convey a great deal of information at a glance. Remember that cost savings for consumers and profit and efficiency for businesses are prime appeals.

- The most successful ads use a large illustration with a headline below it and two or three columns of copy beneath the head.

- Don't split the headline or leave too wide a gutter between columns of copy.

- For ads less than a page, use a vertical page placement.

- Within the layout use diagonals to emphasize motion, power and speed; verticals to imply dominance, power, dignity, and strength; horizontals to imply rest and tranquility, or solidity and trust.

- Be sensitive to the psychological implications of colors and use them to grab the reader and enhance the product benefit. Know color preferences of various target markets.

- Create a natural eye path. The illustration should lead to the headline, especially the benefit and/or product name, down into the body copy, and out through the logo.

- Always align elements for a cleaner design.

- Use a serif typeface in the body copy for better readability.

- Don't use wrap-around copy unless you're willing to sacrifice readership. Keep flush left-hand margins.

- Bleed ads can get very high impact, and generally get higher readership, but in nonbleed ads use a hairline frame of border tape to get a more finished look and to help pull the elements together.

- Never let copy "bleed" to the edge of the page. It will get lost in the fold or clipped off. Leave at least a one-quarter-inch border between print and the outside edge.

- Put the logotype at the bottom middle or bottom right of the layout. Make it large enough to achieve recognition.

Illustration

- Use the illustration to stop the reader and create interest in the product. Suggest a story—i.e., leave something for the reader to fill in through his or her imagination.

- Use the illustration as a visualization of the product benefit, preferably by showing either the product in action or the end result of using it.

- Use a single, dominant illustration rather than multiple visuals.

- Use a photograph rather than a drawing when you can. Photographs are more like perceived reality, therefore more convincing. The less abstract the better for both consumer and business ads. Don't combine photographs and sketches in a single ad.

- Don't run a picture without a caption. Captions have extremely high readability.

- Don't use reverse type or run copy over the illustration.

Typography

- Don't use type purely as a design feature. If it isn't easily readable, it won't communicate the product message.

- Don't use light type; black on white is easier to read. Use light backgrounds in illustrations, and make sure there is enough contrast for the product to stand out clearly. And don't print over the illustration.

- Keep the typeface continuous; never use more than three. Some experts advise using no more than two, with one of them being a serif face for the body copy. Sans serif is okay for headlines, but use serif in the body copy, because it's more easily read. Use a typeface with ligatures for the same reason.

- Don't use color to call out a particular word in the headline or copy. It makes a design out of something which should be read.

- Choose the best typeface on the basis of the product personality and the creative approach. Make sure they all work together for impact and product image consistency.

- Don't use all capital letters in the headline. Lower case makes words easier to read. Capitalize only as you would in a usual sentence.

- Use 10–12-point type for body copy, with 2-point leading for best readability.

- Don't use more than forty characters per column. After this lines begin to "wave" and your reader may not find the beginning of the next line easily enough to keep on reading.

- If you put in a coupon, make sure the print is in a readable face and size, especially if your target market is over 40 years old and may need bifocals. Also be sure to position it on the layout so that it is easily clipped out by the reader.

- Don't: l e t t e r s p a c e   or   wordspace, like this. Keep everything tight and use kerning.

Copy Guidelines

Headlines

- Together the illustration and the headline tell the product story. Use the headline to get attention and to state the product name and benefit. Always appeal directly to the reader's self-interest.

- Lead the reader naturally into the body copy, but never be clever at the expense of the sell. Remember that odds are that most of the body copy will never be read.

- When the headline extends to more than one line, break it so that phrases are kept together as units of thought; don't separate adjectives from the nouns they modify and don't split infinitives or prepositional phrases. When in doubt, check your grammar book.

- Use the product name and a specific benefit in the headline. Numbers in the headline, especially relating to price, have strong appeal.

- News headlines for new products or new uses have strong inherent reader interest.

- When the headline is two or more lines, divide it keeping phrases and words together that naturally belong together.

- Don't split the headline, placing part of it at the top of the page and part elsewhere.

• Don't slant the headline in the layout without good reason.

Body copy

• Start the sell immediately—don't wait. Forget puffery and empathy. Be informative and give the consumer enough facts to believe the headline promise. Remember, being conversational in tone doesn't mean rambling on or being verbose.

• Write enough copy, but don't overwrite. Take out anything extra, but leave out nothing necessary to the message. Don't shy away from long headlines or body copy, however. If the consumer will want or need an explanation or information, especially in technical or business ads, include it.

• Never decorate. Avoid piling up adjectives. Rely on crisp, clear, strong nouns and verbs. Avoid abstract nouns and superlative adjectives.

• Keep a rhythm and balance in your writing, so the copy flows smoothly. Use links between sentences and whole ideas.

• Make sure the copy states
—what the product is,
—what it will do for you,
—where to get it,
—what it costs (prices for retail; suggestion through layout, illustration, and typeface, if not).

• Ask for a response at the end of your copy. For a hard sell, take a "do-it-now" approach. For a soft sell, suggest a change in attitude or planning. In either case, tell the reader what you want him or her to do after reading the ad.

• Always direct the reader where to go for purchase and/or more information.

• Break up long copy with subheads. Use numbers with lists; bold face with subheads.

• Use the present tense.

• Use singular nouns and verbs.

• Use active voice. Avoid passive voice entirely—it weakens any message.

(E.g., it is much more meaningful to say "I love you" than to say "You are loved by me.")

- Use contractions. People speak in them.

- Use proper punctuation, no exclamations. Avoid dots and dashes.

- Involve the reader. Write as if you were talking to a specific person you know, friendly but concise. Use direct address ("you") and words and phrases familiar to your target market. Beware of clichés, sexist and other stereotypic language, and don't talk down to your audience.

- Beware of connotations. Avoid slang.

- Vary sentence and paragraph length.

- Indent paragraphs.

- Always use the most specific, most exact and most sensuous, image-provoking word as well as the most specific, exact facts. Don't settle for the general or the "close-enough."

- Support the improbable with evidence. Avoid any exaggeration. Understate rather than overstate.

- Check spelling and grammar carefully. Be aware of the most commonly misspelled words and always proofread.

- Check the copy fit against the layout space.

9

The Job Interview

Know about the advertising agency or company and their work before you send your résumé or request an interview

To begin, build a mailing list. Go to the library and find the major indexes related to advertisers and agencies and trade publication client/agency locators. Find out who does what and use "the Red Books"—the *Standard Directory of Advertising Agencies* and the *Standard Directory of Advertisers*—to write directly to the person at the highest level of the hiring decision process. Avoid personnel offices and go directly to the top. Your letter will "trickle down" to the appropriate person who will hire you, but chances are, it won't percolate up.

Learn about the company, or who the agency's clients are, and review their ads, so you know their work and can discuss it intelligently. State specifically in your letter why you want to work for that particular agency or company. Give an honest and sincere answer. If you can't come up with one, don't apply.

Remember that advertising is only one part of the communications industry as a whole, and that your skills in advertising are applicable in other areas as well. So when you search for a job, think about in-house advertising in retail stores, public relations departments and agencies, media production departments and houses, printers, radio and television stations. Remember, too, to consider public service institutions, schools, government agencies, nonprofit civic organizations—any group that has to get a message out or to keep up a positive relationship with the public.

State a specific and concise job objective

Know what you want to do and why before you apply. Don't expect someone else to tell you what you want to do. Review job descriptions beforehand. Know salary levels and be generally informed about the advertising business and the position before you go for the interview. This information is available in various advertising textbooks and in general and trade publications in libraries.

Remember that your résumé, your book, and the interview are advertisements of your capabilities

Don't make mistakes in your correspondence, résumé, or book that you wouldn't make in an ad—e.g., don't be cute, get gimmicky, or be general or abstract. Be truthful, straight, informed, and concrete in your approach and what you have to offer.

This doesn't mean you can't be creative, any more than advertising without gimmicks has to be dull. Be creative in your approach and layout, but don't make the form or delivery of your résumé so gimmicky that it will keep the whole creative department laughing for hours. Include a photocopy or photograph of your best ad, or even a tape of a commercial, if you wish—this will show your creativity in its most professional light. But don't have them delivered in a pizza box.

Always send a cover letter, addressed specifically to the person by his or her name and position.

Write your résumé using the same rules you would to write good copy. First, itemize jobs you've had, what you've done in college or on the job that is applicable to what your employer would want you to do, and what responsibilities you've handled. Eliminate the clutter. Forget modesty and realistically assess all your strengths and weaknesses. Then prioritize your list according to your employer's self-interest and write it up with the agency's or company's interests in mind.

Keep it at one page unless you have additional **significant** things to say (everyone expects you to say your health is excellent) and use a format which simply and clearly reveals your "key benefits." If you have outside interests and activities relevant to your work ability that show a sense of responsibility, experience in advertising, or skill in working closely with people, include it.

As you write, emphasize your strengths and inform the reader of what you **can do**. Never let the emphasis rest on names, dates, or titles. If you are a student, be sensitive to the fact that course content is not readily apparent to other people. Don't just give them the name of the course; tell them what you did or learned in it, if it's relevant to what they want to hear. Include such items as press kits, ad campaigns, consumer research projects, etc. Always remember the self-interest of your reader. If you've been in the field for a while, include the specific accounts you've worked on and the responsibilities you've had in relation to them.

If you have a job description to work with, write your résumé to fill it. Rewrite your résumé and have it run off on a laser printer every time you apply for a different job, instead of having the résumé typeset. Keep the format flexible and never settle for a generic résumé when you really want a specific job at a particular company or agency.

See Illustration 9.1 for a **sample résumé** illustrating how job objective as headline and jobs and academic coursework as key selling benefits can be used to advertise yourself through your résumé.

Stay active in the interview process

Call after you send your résumé to set up the interview. State specifically **when** you will call in your cover letter.

Prepare for your interview by

- researching the specific agency or company;

- mentally exploring every aspect of the creative work in your portfolio;

- composing a list of key agency aspects to remember and questions on such areas as chances for advancement, job policies and expectations, basic health benefits, etc.;

- anticipating questions which will be asked of you;

- and mentally reviewing an imaginary film of exactly how you want the interview to progress, over and over.

Good hiring prospects will appear confident, open, and genuinely enthusiastic about their own creative work and that of the agency. They let the interviewer know they are knowledgeable, seriously interested, and concerned about fitting comfortably into the agency or company. They are alive with interests and responsiveness, and they know as much as possible about the concern's practices before the interview.

Neil Vanover, of Tatham-Laird & Kudner, summarizes beautifully what creative directors look for when you walk in the door with your portfolio:

"I look for character and experience. What has the applicant done? What kind of person is he or she? How does he present himself in person and in his work?

"I look for proficiency and skill. How well has the applicant learned our business? How well has she learned from school as well as from studying advertising in print and on broadcast? How well trained is he?

"I look for talent and pray for a spark of genius. Even though the applicant presents him- or herself well and demonstrates an honest grasp of the business, it is difficult to hire him or her unless there is something there that knows how to break the rules, how to create a pattern and then destroy it, how to leap out of the pit with a single bound."

To this, Louis Miano, director of creative services for AC & R, adds the personal quality of "confidence without abrasiveness." John Chervokas, of Sudler & Hennessey, listens for "the strategic idea behind each ad, and the creator being able to speak passionately about the work."

Sometimes an interviewer who is not so astute may ramble on, ask vague questions, or neglect to give you feedback or clues about what is expected. In this case, you will have to look for openings to ask questions and discuss your work. But be polite and unintrusive about doing it.

During the interview, be natural and responsive. Sit toward the edge of the chair, listen carefully and respond. Stay alert. Be prepared to explain why they should hire you. Don't expound egotistically, but don't understate your talents. To be effective, you must sell yourself and make yourself memorable.

This is no time to drag out the "virtue" of self-effacement. If you don't show them why they should hire you, no one else is going to.

Dress and act appropriately to the job—and notice everything

Your personal appearance and the way you act is like an advertising illustration. Dress for your interviews so that you look as if you would fit into the

Amory S. Ward
30 Clear Mountain Road
Boston, MA 02153
(617) 000-000

Objective: An entry level position as a junior copywriter.

Education: B.A., Boston College, Chestnut Hill, MA: May, 1989.
                 Double Major: Communications and English. GPA: 3.3.

Work
Experience: Internship in Creative Services for Jerado & Company
                 Advertising Agency of Boston. Responsibilities included: writing
                 press releases, proofreading copy, pasteup. Participated in
                 creative sessions, client meetings. 1988.

                 Assistant to the Marketing Director, Norris Corporation,
                 Biscayne, FL. Responsibilities included word processing,
                 telemarketing, correspondence. Assisted in organization and
                 distribution of a direct mail promotional campaign for the Norris
                 Education Center. Summer 1985, 1986.

                 Volunteer worker for City Councilman John Burke: assisted in
                 the design and distribution of newspaper ads, door-to-door
                 circulars, direct mail; schedule planning.

Relevant
Course Work: Honors in all communications courses, including: Advertising
                 Survey, Copy and Layout, Public Relations: development of
                 speculative advertising plans; execution of ads in all major print
                 media; promotion planning and development of press kits.
                 Broadcast writing: scripting. Sales and Promotion; Photography;
                 Grammar, Composition.

                 Broadcast journalist for WZBC-FM 90.3. Responsible for
                 researching, organizing wire stories, writing news scripts, on-air
                 delivery. 1986, 1987.

Other: Contributing editor for *BC World*, feature articles; college
                 yearbook; layout and production; fluency in Spanish; BC Ski
                 Team; dorm representative; volunteer writing tutor; World
                 Hunger Committee.

Illustration 9.1 Sample Résumé. The principle of advertising your product's
key benefits should be applied to advertising yourself in your résumé as well.

agency or company naturally and comfortably. When in doubt about what is normal, inconspicuously go there first and see what people wear as they go into work. Remember, though, different jobs require different dress. Account executives don't dress the same as art directors or copywriters.

Arrive early for your interview, and plan for the unexpected to delay you. Use the restroom in anticipation of not seeing it for a few hours more. While you wait, listen to what people say about their work and about others'. Notice attitudes and responses. See what they do and how they appear to feel about it. Talk to people.

If you don't like what you hear or see, use the interview to ask discreetly about your concerns and to practice your interviewing skills. Get as much information as you need to determine whether or not you really want the job.

Get feedback on your book

Above all, get feedback on your book. The more you get, the easier it will be to put it in perspective. Review "Understanding Criticism" in Chapter 3 to make sure you interpret criticism for what is meant, rather than in terms of what you want to hear. Again, never leave an interview without getting a second interview or at least some guidance on improving your portfolio. Use each interview to discover more and more nuances of effective advertising, revising your work each time according to your own common sense and creative judgment.

Watch for developing patterns of criticism rather than jumping on minor changes, and when you've substantially changed some of your weaker ads into strong ones, call back the creative director—or whoever interviewed you. State that you have appreciated his or her suggestions, revised your ads, and would appreciate the opportunity to get feedback on the changes.

At the second round of criticism, be sure to leave your résumé and copies of one or two of your best ads or a single campaign with the person who will make the hiring decision, so that the agency or company can make the connection between your name and your work easily. Make sure everything is properly labeled and provide a folder to keep it all together. Looking professional is already accomplishing one-third of your goal.

Follow up

Send a personalized note after the interview and refer specifically to the content of the interview.

Keep in touch with your agencies and companies of choice, even if there is no immediate vacancy. Write or call or both to let them know you're still interested and ask to be kept in mind. Keep up with what they're doing. **Make friends with secretaries and receptionists.**

If the job market is extremely tight, find out what positions are available and take one which will get your foot in the door but not cut you off from any hope of moving into your desired position. Wherever you go, ask the variety of people you'll come in contact with how they got the jobs they hold and how long they've been in them.

As you go through the rounds of interviews and portfolio building and revising, remember that both the interview and the portfolio are equally important advertisements of you, ads that, if successful, will motivate them to "buy" what you're selling. Ken Lavey, chairman/creative director of Lavey-/Wolff/Swift, cautions: "The first impression you make with your portfolio is *you*, never forget it; that impression is often what determines who gets the job, especially when two portfolios are equally great. The portfolio itself must show your very best work in the cleanest, the simplest, and the most organized way possible."

"MOST IMPORTANT," says Susan Puzzuoli of McCann-Erickson, a twenty-four-year advertising veteran, "Don't give up trying to land that first job. It's a tough field to get into, but once you do, you're hooked. GOOD LUCK."

I couldn't have said it better myself.

Suggested Readings

Trade Journals

Advertising Age
740 Rush Street
Chicago, IL 60611

ADWEEK
820 Second Avenue
New York, NY 10017

Books

Book, Albert and C. Dennis Schick. *Fundamentals of Copy & Layout*. Lincolnwood, Ill.: NTC Business Books, 1987.

Broadbent, Simon, ed. *The Leo Burnett Book of Advertising*. London: Hutchinson, 1984.

Burton, Philip Ward and Scott Purvis. *Which Ad Pulled Best?* Lincolnwood, Ill.: NTC Business Books, 1987.

Caples, John. *Tested Advertising Methods*. Englewood Cliffs, N.J.: Prentice Hall, 1981.

Crow, Wendell C. *Communication Graphics*. Englewood Cliffs, N.J.: Prentice Hall, 1981.

Della Famina, Jerry. *From Those Wonderful Folks Who Gave You Pearl Harbor*. New York: Simon & Schuster, 1970.

Flesch, Rudolph. *The Art of Plain Talk*. New York: Collier MacMillan, 1962.

Higgins, Denis. *The Art of Writing Advertising*. Lincolnwood, Ill.: NTC Business Books, 1987. (Originally published 1965.)

Hopkins, Claude. *Scientific Advertising*. Lincolnwood, Ill.: NTC Business Books, 1986. (Originally published 1953.)

Jewell, A. Jerome. *Creative Strategy in Advertising*, 3rd ed. Belmont, Cal.: Wadsworth Publishing, 1989.

Mogel, Leonard. *Making It in the Media Professions*. Chester, Conn.: Globe Pequot Press, 1988.

Moriarty, Sandra. *Creative Advertising*. Englewood Cliffs, N.J.: Prentice Hall, 1985.

Ogilvy, David. *Confessions of an Advertising Man*. New York: Atheneum, 1984.

————. *Oglivy on Advertising*. New York: Vintage, 1985.

Reeves, Rosser. *Reality in Advertising*. New York: Alfred Knopf, 1961.

Reis, Al and Jack Trout. *Positioning: The Battle for Your Mind*. New York: McGraw-Hill, 1981.

Strunk, William and E. B. White. *Elements of Style*. New York: Macmillan, 1979.

Surmanek, Jim. *Media Planning: A Quick and Easy Guide*. Lincolnwood, Ill.: NTC Business Books, 1985.

Young, James Webb. *How to Become an Advertising Man*. Lincolnwood, Ill.: NTC Business Books, 1987. (Originally published 1963.)

Glossary/Index

Account services Division of an advertising agency that deals directly with the client.

Ad campaign Series of related ads targeted to a specific audience, successively scheduled in different media and designed to achieve a specific product-message impact. (See pp. 7, 9, 10, 13, 76.)

Ad plan An applied ad strategy coordinating target market, message, and media. (See Ill. 1.1.)

Ad strategy A competitive plan for persuading a particular target market to take a specific action or adopt an attitude change. (See Ill. 1.1; p. 3.)

Art director Agency creative responsible for all of the visual artwork of the advertisement, working in conjunction with the copywriter who writes the text. (See pp. 2, 22, 43.)

Bleed Extension of an ad illustration to the trim edge of the page. (See pp. 9, 94.)

Body copy Text of the ad, apart from the headline, usually set in 10–12-point type. (See pp. 3, 9, 31, 33, 35, 41, 43, 46, 60, 68, 77, 81–82, 86–89, 92–98.)

Boldface Heavy, black type. (See pp. 43, 97.)

Book A portfolio of creative advertising work, in ad industry lingo. (See pp. 1–10, 13–18, 21, 25–27, 35, 43, 65, 70, 75, 100, 104.)

Brag and boast An advertising appeal based on a company achievement rather than on a consumer benefit. (See pp. 29, 88, 93.)

Burnisher A stemlike tool with a curved, rounded head used to transfer press type from its holding sheet and then to affix it permanently by rubbing over the letters with a waxy sheet supplied with the lettering. (See p. 41.)

Caption Brief description set immediately adjacent to the photograph or illustration to which it refers. (See p. 95.)

Car card Print ad mounted on the interior wall of a transit vehicle. (See pp. 8, 9, 66–68.)

Cliché An expression so overused that it has lost its impact (See pp. 18, 20, 98.)

Client side Ad agency term referring to the advertiser who hires the agency.

Closure Completion of a suggested figure along lines suggested within it, or the coming together of all elements into a whole that makes sense. (See pp. 73–76, 86, 89.)

Clutter Number of elements fighting for attention. (See pp. 3, 5, 6, 22, 58, 68, 76, 79–89, 93, 100.)

Color separation Process in full-color photography that breaks down the image into its four basic colors—red, blue, yellow, and black. (See p. 82.)

Comprehensive ("comp"). Layout which resembles as closely as possible the appearance of the finished ad. (See Ill. 4.5, 4.6; p. 33.)

Continuous tone (line drawing). Black-and-white drawing with no shades of grey.

Copy Text of the advertisement. (See pp. 82, 85, 87, 88, 92, 94–98. See **Body copy** also.)

Copy fit Exact space occupied by the copy text. (See pp. 43, 98.)

Copy sheet Sheet mounted on the back of, or adjacent to, a "semi-comp" or "comp" which identifies client and media, credits art and copy, and includes headline and body copy, with printer specifications. (See Ill. 4.9; pp. 43, 65.)

Copywriter Agency creative responsible for writing the text for an ad, in conjunction with the art director who does the visual artwork. (See pp. 2, 22, 41, 43, 104.)

Cost per Thousand (CPM). Cost of reaching 1,000 people with a media message.

Creative Person involved in preparing artwork or copy for an advertisement.

Creative strategy or platform Plan and rationale for an ad or campaign specifically designed to capture the attention and interest of a designated target market. (See pp. 8, 10, 16, 22, 60, 74.)

Demographics Vital statistics including age, sex, income, etc., of a specified group. (See p. 88.)

Direct mail Advertising delivered directly to the target market through the mail. (See pp. 9, 48–58.)

Display type Type larger than 12-point body copy type, used for headlines and key words and phrases in other parts of the layout.

Downscale Targeted toward lower socioeconomic groups.

Editorial environment Image associated with a particular medium which "rubs off" onto the product or service advertised. (See pp. 9, 60.)

Eye path Movement of the eye as it scans the page, stopping at various points, and moving on, according to reader interest or as planned and directed by the layout of elements on the page. (See pp. 72, 76, 94.)

Figure In Gestalt psychology, the shape of a thing that stands out as a whole against a more diffuse or vague background or "nonthing." (See pp. 77, 81–82, 87.)

Flush (left or right). Aligned in a straight column, left or right. (See p. 94.)

Focus group Group interview designed to elicit consumer opinion on a specific product or concept. (See p. 31.)

Font A complete alphabet of a specific typeface and point size. (See Ill. 4.7.)

Free-lance Referring to work done by a professional outside an agency or company. (See p. 1.)

Free-standing insert (FSI). Preprinted ad inserted into a print publication.

Generic Without an identifying brand name. (See pp. 6, 101.)

Gestalt In Gestalt psychology, a whole which loses its integrity when any part of it is altered in relation to any other part. (See pp. 72–76.)

Good continuation In Gestalt psychology, the completion of a figure or idea according to a pattern established by the whole. (See p. 75.)

Greeking Nonsense type used in an ad "comp" to indicate the final appearance of the ad when copy is typeset. (See Ill. 4.5; pp. 33–35.)

Gross rating point (GRP). Measure of total audience exposure to a media message.

Ground In Gestalt psychology, the vague and undefined backdrop against which a figure may be perceived. (See pp. 77, 81, 82.)

Halftone Process that breaks down the shades of grey in a photograph into black dots of varying sizes, to give the impression of grey when the dot is seen against the white space that surrounds it.

Hard sell A strong, direct, and immediate appeal to purchase based on argument. (See p. 97.)

Head Headline. (See pp. 33, 41, 46, 75, 81, 85–89, 96–97.)

Illustration Artwork or photography used in an advertisement. (See pp. 8, 23, 33, 35, 41, 45, 60, 65, 66, 68, 80–89, 95.)

Image ad Ad whose selling point is based on a projected personality rather than a specific product benefit. (See pp. 16, 48, 53.)

Italic Type slanted slightly to the right. (See Ill. 4.7; pp. 43, 89.)

Justification (of type). Lettering aligned in a column on both the right and left sides, with spacing distributed evenly between the words on the line. (See p. 43.)

Key benefit (product or consumer). Product characteristic seen as the most meaningful by the prospective consumer. (See p. 101.)

Layout Planned arrangement of all the elements included in an ad. (See Ill. 4.1; pp. 33–35, 43–46, 76, 79–89, 91–94.)

Leading Space between lines of type. (See pp. 43, 96.)

Line art (continuous tone). Black-and-white drawing with no shades of grey. (See p. 66.)

Line screen Screen through which a photograph is shot to break it into a series of single tone dots of various size, which then appear as shades of grey in the final print.

Logo (logotype). The name or symbol of the advertiser used consistently in its advertising to achieve company recognition. (See pp. 41, 94.)

Marketing mix System of production, pricing, distribution, and promotion used to market a product.

Media mix Primary and secondary media chosen to advertise a product because of the exposure of the designated target market to it.

Medium Means of communicating the advertising message: newspapers, magazines, direct mail, radio, television, etc. Plural form is **media**. (See pp. 7–10, 46, 47–70.) Also, the means employed in creating an art form: watercolor, oil, pastel, charcoal, etc. Plural form is **mediums**.

Metaphor A figure of speech that makes a direct comparison between two apparently unlike things. (See pp. 21, 23, 66, 77, 84, 87.)

Needs-felt Motivation for product purchase based on desirability. (See pp. 32, 72, 99.)

Needs-real Motivation for product purchase based on necessity. (See p. 32.)

Newsprint Coarse, inexpensive and highly absorbent paper used for newspapers. (See p. 66.)

_____

Outdoor poster Illustrations applied in preprinted sheets to billboards along roads and highways. (See pp. 8, 9, 47–48, 75.)

Overline A subhead placed above and leading into the headline.

_____

Painted bulletin ("paint") Individually painted illustrations on outdoor billboards. (See pp. 8, 9, 47–48.)

Pasteup/mechanical All layout elements are complete, pasted into position, and ready for the camera and platemaking. (See pp. 33–35.)

Perception Process by which we gather information from our environment and determine its meaning. (See pp. 72–87.)

Picas Unit of measure for a column of type. Six picas = one inch.

Point of purchase advertising Any advertising done at the place where the buying decision is made. It may consist of free-standing displays in a supermarket, shelf displays, or even product packaging itself. (See p. 2.)

Point size Height of the type, proportioned seventy-two points to the inch. (See pp. 43, 68, 96.)

Potential consumer One willing and able to buy the product. (See **Target market.**)

Press type/transfer lettering Complete alphabets in specific typeface and point size ready to be rubbed off, giving the appearance of having been typeset. Used for headlines in comprehensive layouts. (See pp. 33–35.)

Product or brand image The complex of associations of life-style, attitudes and values associated with a particular product or name. (See pp. 8, 13, 53, 54, 74, 80, 87.)

Product differentiation Characteristic that distinguishes a product from its competitor. (See pp. 30, 32, 54, 66, 76.)

Product life cycle The natural birth, growth, and death of a product, determined by its market acceptance and sales pattern over time. (See p. 32.)

Product positioning Match between target market need and product image and benefit; place a product or service occupies in the mind of the consumer in relation to its competition. (See pp. 29–32, 60, 70, 72, 74, 80, 85.)

Psychographics Felt needs, values, attitudes, and interests characteristic of the target market.

Repositioning Change in product positioning in terms of user or product benefit. (See p. 13.)

Reverse type Light letters on a dark background. (See pp. 22, 82, 89, 95.)

Rough First stage of ad development after the thumbnail sketch, visualizing the ad's basic elements and layout. (See Ill. 4.3; pp. 14, 33–35, 41.)

Run-of-press (ROP). Placement by convenience of the publisher; color quality defined by the capability of its press. (See p. 66.)

Sans serif Typeface characterized by a lack of flourishes or cross strokes on its letters. (See Ill. 4.7; p. 95.)

Segmentation Subgroups within a whole, defined to determine a potential target market. (See p. 29.)

Selective perception Seeing only what interests us or confirms our own preconceptions; ignoring contradictory information or data irrelevant to our needs. (See p. 79.)

Semi-comprehensive layout ("Semi-comp"). Layout sketched with all final elements of the ad in position and indicated by sketching for the illustration, hand lettering in the headline, and lines for copy. Stage of ad development between a rough and a comprehensive layout. (See Ill. 4.4; pp. 33–35.)

Serif Typeface having letters with a stroke at the top and bottom. (See Ill. 4.7; pp. 94–95.)

Sex sell Use of sex appeal rather than product benefit to draw interest to a product. (See pp. 17, 74.)

Signature Name of the company or product written in a distinctive style and used characterisitically and continuously in advertisements to achieve name recognition. (See Ill. 4.9.)

Soft sell An indirect motivational appeal to create a favorable buying attitude rather than a hard-hitting argument to purchase now. (See p. 97.)

Spec (speculative) **book** Series of original ads and ad campaigns based on either theoretical or actual products or services, done to display one's creative talent. (See pp. 1, 9, 14, 15, 17.)

Spectacular Outdoor billboards with special effects in dimension, lighting, or moving works.

"Starch"ing Evaluation of print ads by reader interview to determine the percentage of readers who noted the ad, associated it with the advertiser's name, and read most of the body copy. Paid service, developed by Daniel Starch. (See p. 79.)

Storyline Plot or element in a tale designed to spark the reader's interest. (See pp. 58, 89.)

Subhead Sectional headline designed to signal key points in the body copy and to break up large blocks of print. (See pp. 41, 97.)

Suffering point Addressing relief of a negative consumer concern, such as chapped hands, as opposed to another benefit, such as a choice of colors. (See pp. 16, 66, 68.)

Surprinting Printing over an illustration rather than a blank background. (See p. 89.)

Symbolism Use of concrete words and images to suggest another meaning or intangible idea. (See pp. 21, 23, 41, 72, 80, 81, 85.)

Synecdoche Symbolic use of a part to stand for the whole, as in "the crown" to refer to the king and his office. (See pp. 86–87.)

Tagline Catchy summary phrase used at the end of an ad to promote memorability of the product or company. (See Ill. 4.9.)

Target market Best potential consumer for a particular product, determined by ability to appreciate the product benefit, to afford the product price, and to make or directly influence the buying decision. (See pp. 3, 4, 6, 8, 9, 17, 21, 25, 26, 29, 30, 31–32, 49, 53, 60, 70, 72, 74, 82, 86, 87, 88, 89, 92, 94, 96, 98.)

Thumbnail (sketch). Rough miniature sketch of what the ad will look like in basic design and layout. (See Ill. 4.2; pp. 33, 41.)

Tint block Area colored differently from the rest of the copy background. (See p. 88.)

Trade advertising Advertising directed at retailers and wholesalers.

Typeface Type of lettering chosen for its personality and suitability to the product image. (See Ill. 4.7; pp. 9, 33, 35, 41, 43, 46, 58, 76, 88, 92, 94, 95, 97.)

_____

Upscale Targeted towards upper socioeconomic groups. (See pp. 54, 58, 87.)

_____

Vicarious experience Imagined rather than actual participation in a real event. (See p. 24.)

_____

White space Any space not covered by copy or illustration. (See pp. 66, 93.)

About the Author

Ann Marie Barry, Ph.D., is a communications professor at Boston College and a free-lance copywriter. She holds advanced degrees in advertising, American literature, perceptual psychology, and film. She is a member of Phi Kappa Phi, a former University Scholar at Boston University, a recipient of the NBC National Teacher's Award, and, most recently, an AEF Visiting Professor at DDB Needham Worldwide, New York.